Tempus ORAL HISTORY *Series*

Chelmsford
voices

Grandparents of Douglas Catt.

Tempus ORAL HISTORY *Series*

Chelmsford
voices

Compiled by
Mary Flynn and Diane Watson

TEMPUS

First published 2001
Copyright © Mary Flynn and Diane Watson, 2001

Tempus Publishing Limited
The Mill, Brimscombe Port,
Stroud, Gloucestershire, GL5 2QG

ISBN 0 7524 2202 2

Typesetting and origination by
Tempus Publishing Limited
Printed in Great Britain by
Midway Colour Print, Wiltshire

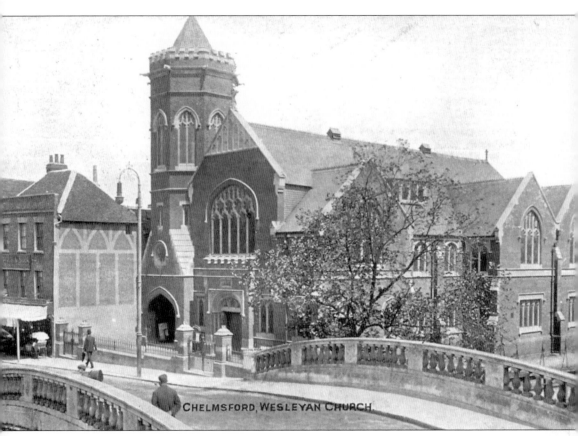

Chelmsford Wesleyan church.

Contents

Westlands boys with Ted Revell.

Introduction

Our research has led us to meet a wide variety of interesting characters who live and have lived in Chelmsford. Most of these have witnessed the many changes that the town has undergone during the last ninety years or so. As well as experiencing the distress and upheaval of the war years, they have witnessed and enjoyed the growing prosperity that comes with thriving industry and new commercial interests.

There has been a settlement on this site since Roman times but the modern town dates from 1199 when King John established Chelmsford as a market town. The people of the late twelfth century could not possibly have imagined that 800 years later the market would still be one of Chelmsford's biggest attractions. Although it is now housed inside, it has remained, like the rivers Chelmer and Cam that still thread their way through the town centre, a constant factor. Chelmsford has an enviable industrial history, being well known for its electronic engineering. Hoffmans, who made ball and roller bearings, were a target of enemy bombs during the Second World War, and Marconi's company which developed radio telegraphy, was also based here. Both of these companies have in the past been major employers of Chelmsford people.

We are both touched by and grateful for the kindness and assistance we received from everyone we spoke to, for the offers of tea and coffee, the fantastic sense of humour which found us chuckling long after we had finished the interview. It was remarkable how many people were lucky enough to enjoy friendships formed at school many years ago, often working and retiring together. The men and women who worked at the big engineering companies described the experience as belonging to a 'family', with social occasions and outings being taken together. The firemen both active and retired also felt they belonged to a 'family'; they are all very proud of the people who worked with them and the tasks they have accomplished.

We have been told by numerous people how much they appreciated the good quality of education and the forward-thinking teachers they encountered in several of the local schools and the Technical College; this obviously was the basis on which was built the academic community, the University Campus, which now has such an important role to play in modern Chelmsford. King Edward VI's Grammar School for boys and the County High School for girls remain excellent bastions of learning.

We have heard how children made their own fun with street games, hikes by the river, cycle rides in the surrounding countryside and opportunities for adventure that the local youth groups offered. Later came the enjoyment of swimming in the open pool, which still exists now and is supplemented by the major new sports and leisure centres. The four old cinemas are now

Olive Catt in The Gondoliers.

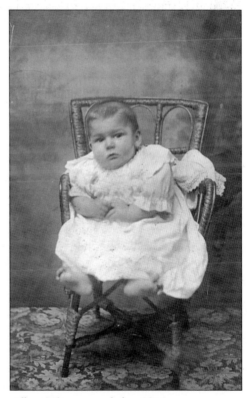

Albert Watson as a baby, 1914.

replaced by a multi-screen complex. The dances at the Corn Exchange and in the Odeon ballroom have long gone and nightclubs have taken their place. The town has grown and expanded its leisure attractions but some of the old sources of entertainment like the Chelmsford Amateur Operatic and Dramatic Society and the yearly carnival remain. People have vivid memories especially of Carnival Day when the parade had finished and they spent a summer's night dancing by the river.

Prior to television, it seems to us, more people actively took part in sport and supported their local football and cricket teams at the weekends. The cricket ground which stages County cricket is renowned for being the best-kept ground in Essex. Unfortunately for many the days of cheering on their local football side at its town centre ground have been lost.

Religion played an important part in everyday life, in school, in youth activities and in festivals. Each denomination also enjoyed full attendance at their Sunday services and Sunday schools, many of the children walking a long way several times during the day. There are some references to and happy memories of the fifteenth-century Cathedral, especially from those who were married there over the years and the members of the Cathedral choir. Its annual highlight is now the Annual Cultural Festival which takes place in May.

As a market town both past and present the sights and sounds of the stallholders is an integral part of any shopping trip. Of course mothers no longer take their children to see the animals but almost everything else is still available; although you can still buy materials and sewing aids you are more likely to see a display of ready-made clothes. In Moulsham Street there is still an aura of yesteryear where little shops jostle each other for space. In the town centre the shops that people remember with affection like Smith, Bonds and Liptons are no longer there. Gradually the townspeople have extended their shopping facilities to include High Chelmer and the Meadows as well as peripheral retail parks. People born in the first half of the twentieth century are learning to appreciate modern conveniences but still retain a nostalgia for the closer communities of Chelmsford past.

We would like to thank everybody who has helped us with our research and kindly trusted us with their precious family photographs. We are particularly indebted to Lynne Harding, who gave us access to Chelmsford Fire Brigade archives; Douglas Catt who loaned us unique photographs from his childhood as well as an insight into the early days of the Chelmsford Amateur Operatic and Dramatic Society; Dennis Smith, Ted Revell and others who brought to life their early days on the shop floor; also special thanks to Molly Watson for her humour. It was a pleasure as well as an honour to talk to the townsmen and women and to share their personal memories. We hope everyone will get as much pleasure from reading this book as we had in writing it.

Mary Flynn and Diane Watson
April 2001

CHAPTER 1

Home

Douglas Catt aged five years.

The Youell Family

All of my grandparents lived in Chelmsford. Both grandads were 'horse men' – Grandad Youell on the farm in Waterhouse Lane, where the barn still stands but is now a Managers' Conference Room in the entrance to Marconi, Waterhouse Lane. He lived in one of the two still standing cottages in Waterhouse Lane. They lived there when it was only a lane and was surrounded by fields and Waterhouse Lane was only a dirt track and it used to flood.

Grandad Cornell worked for Marriages and I think Moy's Coal. He lived in Railway Street; the cart horses used to be lined up there waiting to be loaded or waiting for grandad Cornell to come out of the Ship pub (or so I'm told!).

Bert Youell

St John's Avenue

We bought our house in St John's Avenue when the properties were newly built. The builder was Mr Gozzet. Number 17 has been our home ever since. In 1955 I got a job at Chapman's the jewellers in the High Street, then trained to be a telephonist for the GPO. I worked as a supervisor, finally being in charge at Maldon, but until 1978 I worked in the main exchange behind the Cathedral.

Grace Pheasant

Mill Road

I was born in 1924 at Mill Road where Townfield Street car park is now; right against the railway line and near Ridley's Mill which was burnt down around 1969. Later after we had moved from Mill Lane in the early part of the war a bomb hit the street and the house was demolished; it was occupied then by the lady who was employed as cook at the fire station. She and her mother came to Chelmsford from London, and both were killed.

Pete Huckle

My Wife Doris

I was called up by the RAF and served from 1943 until 1946. My training as an instrument repairer was in Yorkshire and from there I travelled over to France, through Europe to Germany before being demobbed in 1946. I returned to Chelmsford and my job with Chelmsford Fire Brigade and met my wife Doris Edna Halls, who came from Writtle, during a dance at the Corn Exchange in Tindal Square. We were married on August 11th 1947. Doris wore a traditional white dress and my twin sisters who were our bridesmaids wore pink satin. When we first got married we lived at 21 Townfield Street, a two-up two-down house which is still standing. Our first child was born while we lived there; our second son was born after we bought our second home in Fairfield Road. The second house cost us £1,700 but it was a bigger house with three bedrooms. Our two sons David and Michael were raised there; they went to the C. of E. School in Victoria Road. We lived there for twenty-one years before moving to Kelvedon. Doris and I occasionally went to the cinema: we liked Disney films the best. We went more often to the Corn Exchange to dance to the music of the big bands. It cost 1s 6d or 2s to go to the cinema and a little more to go to the Corn Exchange. A lot of big bands came to Chelmsford including Joe Louis and Ted Heath.

Harold Wakelin

Hard Housework

Women worked very hard in the house when I was a child. I can remember seeing my mother cleaning the windows upstairs – she was sat on the concrete windowsill with her legs inside and the sash window pulled down on her lap. she held on with one hand and cleaned the windows with the other. There was a concrete boiler built into the corner of the kitchen where all the linen was boiled before being rinsed in the sink. It was heavy work, especially putting it all through the mangle before hanging it on the line. In the winter the washing froze on the line – it was a peculiar sight. My mother went shopping each day and carried everything back. She was a wonderful cook and we had fresh food always. We didn't have a Hoover or carpets and Mum seemed to be always sweeping and washing the floors.

Mary Scott

Almost Requisitioned

Houses were hard to come by just after the war but we were so lucky because someone came into my father's shop and mentioned that he was going over the road to Cobb & Wincer, the estate agents opposite. My father said 'Don't go, I'm looking for a house', so Father bought it and we paid him rent. The house was in Henry Road and after we signed for it Bernard decided to camp there for a week. On the day we moved in at the end of that week, someone from the Council came and asked if it was inhabited, as the property had been rebuilt after being bombed during one of the raids on Hoffmans. If Bernard hadn't been there it would have been requisitioned for people who had been made homeless by the bombing, so we were lucky again.

Mary Woolf

His Wife's Big Hat

My husband came from Writtle and I met him during the war at a Corn Exchange dance when he was home on leave from the Kings Own Scottish Borderers. I married in 1948 in the North Avenue Congregational church. I wore a white frock made by a little old lady in Hill Road. I had my cousin Jean and my friend Hilda as bridesmaids and the reception was held in Cannons Restaurant in Victoria Road. Because of the petrol shortage a single-decker bus was hired to carry relatives and guests from the church to the reception. Someone my father knew was going on holiday and offered to drive us to Walton-on-the-Naze for our honeymoon. Peter and I sat in the back of this tiny Austin 7 while the driver's wife who happened to be wearing a very big hat sat next to her husband in the front. We came back by train.

Mary Ellis

Rainsford Avenue

I was born in 1913 and have always been told that I suffered ill health until I was about one year old. After their marriage my parents had built a home in Rainsford Avenue where we lived until after the First World War, moving during the '20s to the accommodation above the Moulsham Street shop. Also during the First World War we had spent some time living with my grandparents Underwood at 38 Dukes Street. One of my early memories is of E. Payne's photography business in Duke Street, almost opposite Fairfield Road. I went there as a young child to have my photograph taken.

Douglas Catt

Longstomps Avenue

After school we often stayed at each other's houses. I stayed with Jennifer Mussell, she lived in Longstomps Avenue. We would sometimes play tennis on the courts at

Bert Youell with his brother and grandfather.

1925. The nursing home was by the river. My earliest memory is of being pushed in my pram: I was sitting up and the hood was up and I was being taken for a walk in Central Park.

We lived at No. 2 Hall Street which was my grandfather's house. My father took over my grandfather's business, a music shop in Moulsham Street – the building is still there. When my grandfather retired we moved to the accommodation above the shop. We believe that many years before, the building had been a girls' school and was later divided into two, as we discovered an interconnecting door. It was fun living there; there were four cellars, three dark and one with some light as it had a window. It is a possibility that at one time this was the servants' quarters, as one of the cellars contained a 'range'. I played down there and of course we kept the coal there as well.

Phyllis Everett

Oakland Park. Maybe I would stay with Valerie Dines who lived in the houses behind Broomfield Hospital where her father worked. You had to walk through a small copse to get there, passing the place where someone kept pigs in sties – it was creepy in the late evening. Rosemary Peacock lived in Norton Mandeville, a small village outside Chelmsford and towards Ongar.

Diane Watson

Central Park

I was born in Chelmsford in what used to be a nursing home on the London Road in

Ice like Sheets of Glass

I was born in Chelmsford in 1922. I had two sisters and I was the one in the middle. As children we grew up in Woodland Road. My mother came from Nottingham and my father from Berkshire; he came to Chelmsford to work for Thompson's ironmongers who were then situated in Rainsford Road. I got married in 1947 in the Victoria Road Baptist church. From January to March of that year we were snowed under and it just cleared in time for the wedding. That was a winter – the roads were iced over and going along to work at Marconi's the roads were like sheets of glass.

Gladys Hilliard

Fairfield Close

My parents were from Huntingdon; my father was a printer at Duttons in Chelmsford and we lived in Mill Road through to 1938 when we moved to Campbell Close. We moved again to Fairfield Road where we remained throughout the war. During a blitz on Chelmsford, the bus station was hit and it took the roof off our house.

Pete Huckle

Arbour Lane

In 1943 when my husband Bert was serving in the RAF I lived with my two eldest boys in furnished rooms in Prykes Drive. The house was owned by a widower who lived on his own and my duties were to keep the house clean and provide a hot meal each day which he ate with us; because of this the rent was reduced to £3 a month. We shared the living room and the kitchen but had one bedroom to ourselves which we and the children shared together. Bert was posted to Boreham before being sent to Norway and I used to regularly take the children to visit him. I often pushed the babies in their pram along Arbour Lane which was then surrounded with fields to meet him at Boreham. It was a long walk but we were used to walking long distances in those days and anyway there weren't any buses.

Molly Watson

Mabel Rusby

I came to Chelmsford in 1941 when I was three years old. My mother had already died and my father was one of the first Greeks to make his home in this country. My elder brother, my twin brother and I moved to Ockelford Avenue, from Dr Barnardo's at Barking Side where we had been placed after the death of our mother, when we were fostered out to an English family. We lived with my foster mother Mabel Rusby at 21 Ockelford Avenue, her mother and father Mr and Mrs Bill Noakes lived two doors away and they also fostered children from Dr Barnardo's – we called them Grandma and Grandad. Bill Noakes had a horse and cart and went round the streets of Chelmsford selling groceries.

George Christodoulou

Tony, Ray and Norman Watson.

George Christodoulou (left) and his brother at Dr Barnardo's.

Manor Farm

I lived at Manor Farm, a tied farmhouse next to Pennack's undertakers and builders. The farm led down to Baddow Meads and was owned by Mr Carter who had two sons, they also owned farms, they were called the 'Hungry Carters' by villagers because they were so mean. We paid no rent and shared the house with the Ambrose family, the Youngs in the attic and the Ambroses in the cellars, with the middle rooms divided fairly between the two families. There were seven of us children and eighteen children in the Ambrose family.

It was a rambling building and I remember the kitchen sink was a large slab of concrete with a big hole which was directly above the sewer. It had to be kept plugged to prevent rats and mice climbing up. Every Friday father helped mother fill up the tin bath with warm water, it was in front of the fire and he always helped mother bathe the children. As we got bigger he would carry the bath upstairs so we could bathe in private. Father worked from dawn to dusk and also worked in our twenty yards of garden so we were always self-supporting.

Ida Cunningham

The £1,750 House

When I married in 1946 we went to live with my husband's father in Embankment Terrace off Victoria Road where the post office is now. It was a cottage and my father-in-law had it modernized; we later bought it ourselves and lived there for nine years. I had a son and a daughter; Ann was born in Brooklands Nursing Home in London Road where the flats are now, my son was born at St John's. When my daughter was eight and my son four my husband and I bought a new house in Beehive Lane – one of the new buildings built after the war. We paid £1,750 for it and stayed there about six years before moving to Gilmore Way at Great Baddow in about 1960 where we remained.

Doris Wesley

Chignal

My father came from Suffolk to be village blacksmith in Chignal when I was four years old, in 1927. I had two brothers and three sisters and we lived in the cottage next door to the blacksmith's forge. My father made our bikes at the forge but when we left school and started work my mother bought us a brand new bike to cycle to work on. On Saturday nights when we lived in Chignal the tin bath would be put in front of the fire ready for our baths, a stone hot water bottle, filled with boiling hot water, was put in our bed and it would be lovely and warm. The toilet was down the bottom of the garden; as children we were frightened of the dark so mum or dad would stand outside and wait for us.

Ted Revell

Married during the War

I married during the war in 1942 – we had to get a special licence. My wife, Mollie, and

Grandfather Bill Noakes is on the right.

Arthur and Elizabeth Young in 1950.

Alice Rose Revell.

her family came from Feering and we have now been married for fifty-eight years. After travelling on a daily basis into Chelmsford for work we finally moved into the town in 1955. We lived on the Westlands Estate and after seven years we moved to the Meadgate Estate where we lived for the next forty-six years.

Dennis Smith

Steam Everywhere

When we lived at North Avenue in a house built about 1930 I bought mostly second-hand furniture, except for the beds. We had no carpet – it was just lino with scattered rag rugs. We had a bathroom and you had to put 2s 6d in the gas meter to heat enough water for a bath: as you can imagine with three boys I was always running out of half-

crowns. There was always lots of washing to do and we had no machines. There was a big zinc boiler in the scullery which was heated by gas and I used a massive rolling pin to fish the clothes out. There was steam everywhere as everyone did their washing at the same time, you couldn't see North Avenue for steam. The clothes were always lovely and clean and so much whiter than they are today.

Molly Watson

Tulip Pub

I was born in 1918 in Phillips Cottages in Springfield, near to the Tulip pub. My mother and father came from Hastings before the First World War and then the whole family followed them to settle in Chelmsford. Phillips Cottages were a terraced 'L' shape; between us and the Tulip was the Dane family's cottage. The pub had an orchard behind it and in the corner of the 'L' shape was a little sweet shop called Everetts. Now the whole area is built on and it is all housing estates. I was still living in Phillips Cottages at the beginning of the war when a plane came down in the field opposite the Tulip Pub and the pilot was taken prisoner.

Sally Pattendon

Hospital Isolation

When I was five years old I went for a hernia operation in the Chelmsford and Essex Hospital, but unfortunately I caught chickenpox while I was in there. I was so itchy they had to strap me to the bottom of the bed so I wouldn't break the stitches. I was in hospital for five weeks instead of the two weeks I should have been and visitors who came had to see me through a screen. A little boy was in there with a broken leg which he got by falling off the pipes he had been climbing. This happened as Victoria Road was being laid, seventy-eight years ago.

Ivy Holden

Queen of Tonga

When we first got married in Galleywood, we rented rooms for a few years before we moved into a cottage in 1950 where we stayed until 1983. In the mid 1920s a few council houses were built; they were non-estate and had road frontage only. Later, in the early '50s Galleywood and other large estates were developed. Like most people, we used coal for heating; it was delivered by the Co-op coal merchant. Most things were delivered prior to a Co-op starting up in the village. Shopkeepers came around collecting your order for meat and groceries and then came back and delivered everything. Most things came through the Co-op – it was a good service. When our children were small we bought a new pram and pushchair from them. Our first furniture was either utility or good quality second-hand. We also had deliveries by van from other tradesmen of bread, milk, paraffin and other things.

Our main entertainment was listening to the radio. As a child I listened to *Children's Hour* with 'Uncle Mac', Derek McCulloch, and Larry the Lamb. We didn't have electricity until 1936 but listened to an old battery set prior to that. The church set up a television set in 1953 so we could all watch the Queen's Coronation; it was quite a unique event. There were other activities in the village for the Coronation but everyone got soaked as it rained so heavily and we all went home and lit a fire. Surely people must remember seeing the Queen of Tonga sitting upright in her carriage while getting soaking wet!

David Cook

Paraffin Oil Lamps

In Chignal we had paraffin oil lamps, but later on in Corporation Road we had gas lights – we were also pleased to have a bathroom and toilet upstairs. In Chignal we had a boiler in the kitchen for the washing, and in the living room had a range called a 'Kitchener' for cooking. There was a pantry

Harry Revell, blacksmith.

in the corner of the living room where all the food was kept and, like most other families, the front room was kept for special occasions. In the early days we had a 'Christie Brothers Relay', with a speaker in the room and programmes relayed from Christie Brothers. We paid a weekly rental for this.

Ted Revell

Sunrise Avenue

After we were married we stayed with my parents who had by this time moved to Sunrise Avenue. Sadly my mother died three months after our marriage so in the circumstances we remained at Sunrise Avenue for the next thirteen years. My first child was born in 1949 in Brooklands, London Road and in 1953 we had another daughter who was born in the nursing home along the Broomfield Road. We finally had our first home in Nalla Gardens in 1960.

Gladys Hilliard

Moving House

After Thelma and I were married in 1947 we lived with my mother in Fairfield Road for a year. We then moved to a top-floor flat in Hylands House, which had been requisitioned; we were there for six months. In 1949, five days before we had our first child, Cara, we moved to 65 Eastern Crescent off North Avenue to a little house and we moved to our present address in 1952. Our son David and daughter Linda were born in 1952 and 1956 – they all live fairly locally.

Pete Huckle

Mildmay Road

I was born in Mildmay Road in 1921. My mother was born in Moulsham Street and my father came from Buckinghamshire to work at the old Crompton Works. I went to Friars Infants' School when I was five years old (that school no longer exists), and then to the Trinity Road School where I passed my eleven-plus scholarship and went to King Edward VI Grammar School.

Doug Pheasant

Smoke Through the Wall

After we were married we went to live with my husband Peter's parents in Writtle. Just before my son was born we managed to get a cottage in George Street opposite the Select cinema. It was two-up and two-down with a toilet out the back. There was only one door and the neighbours' door was right opposite ours, and the toilet was wedged between Duponts wall and London Road. Peter went down one morning and said, 'There's smoke coming out of the toilet!' so I went round and discovered that it was the old man next door smoking and as the toilets were back to back the smoke was coming through the walls.

Mary Ellis

Four Poster Bed

We got married in 1947 at Chelmsford Cathedral. I wore a silky costume in mushroom pink with a brown and pink hat rakishly over one eye, and a pair of brown shoes; clothes were still on ration. We had a week in Colchester for our honeymoon we went to the George Hotel and slept in a four poster bed, I remember all the confetti over the floor. My husband was Bernard Woolf and he worked in County Hall in the education department for forty years.

Mary Woolf

Iron Cooker

There was a big black iron cooker in the kitchen and a coal fire in the living room. The bedrooms had no means of heating and were icy cold; in the morning there would be frost patterns on the inside of the window panes. We did have a luxury – a stone hot water bottle – but we only had one so it was passed from bed to bed. We always refilled it with hot water before putting it in another bed.

Molly Watson

Pennack Family

Before I went to school and after I had done my paper round I went next door to the Pennacks. Mrs Pennack had rheumatoid arthritis and at 8.30, after her husband had got her out of bed and downstairs, I would help her to wash and dress before I got her breakfast. I was given a bag of cakes on Saturday in payment for my help.

Pete and Thelma Huckle.

19

The young Molly Watson.

They had a huge garden with a big quince tree in it; the fruit was very sour. The garden was full of daffodils and tulips which surrounded four or five beehives. Mrs Pennack was horrified of bees and would send me into the garden to pick the flowers for her. My father who had kept bees when he was younger told me to talk to the bees; also if anyone died it had to be reported to the bees, so I told them all the news. I was never frightened and I never got stung. I think the Pennacks sold the honey – I know we didn't get any of it. Dr Spencer Phillips lived near the Blue Lion. He was very tall, bald as a badger and his head was covered in freckles. He was very nice and so was his wife who would tell us to help ourselves to windfalls. He had two sisters who were old

maids and who lived with him. There were two other families that lived opposite the Blue Lion, the Byfords and the Rankins. I sometimes ran errands for them and got a copper or two in return.

Ida Cunningham

Cathedral Wedding

I left Hoffmans in 1946 when I was getting married, although my husband still worked there in J Dept. He was there for over forty years; having started as an apprentice he worked his way up to the position of foreman. I got married in Chelmsford Cathedral on May 18th 1946. Canon Morrow married us and I remember it was a long walk up the aisle. I wore a white dress which I had saved my clothing coupons for, two of my work mates were bridesmaids and we had the reception at the County Hotel. We went to Bournemouth for our honeymoon on the train – all the guests came to the platform to wave us off and as was the custom then the train also gave us a 'toot'.

Doris Wesley

Ruth Lodge

When I was in Writtle I had two brothers, one who died young, and a sister. Our house was called Roman House in the big garden at the side were the green houses called Saltmarsh Nurseries where we grew everything. Roman House was later sold and we built another home on the nursery land so I lived among the flowers, so to speak. We had a live-in maid who met us from school and got our tea; she then looked after us until my parents came home. She would sit in the kitchen and she taught me to knit and sew. Her name was Ruth Lodge and she was with us from when I was aged five to seven when she left. Ruth returned to us at a later date.

Mary Woolf

Tramps and Billy Cans

Mrs Hines our next-door neighbour was a kindly old soul. Tramps would go to her door and she would find something for them and she would also fill their billy cans; they never knocked on any other door but hers. We stayed over a year in George Street and then moved to Hunts Drive in Writtle. We later swapped houses with someone from The Green and we were very happy there.

Mary Ellis

Lionfield Terrace

I was born in Lionfield Terrace in Springfield in the year 1917. My mother came from Strood in Rochester and my father came from Walmer in Kent. My mother came to Chelmsford when she was only thirteen years old to look after her great-grandfather and my father was a shop assistant, I think he worked at the Co-op. They met at a church in Baddow Road and my younger brother and I were both born in Chelmsford. We had three rooms downstairs and three bedrooms also a little garden, the front parlour was shut up and we only went in there at Christmas time or

for parties. We had a tin bath and an outside toilet.

Ivy Holden

Beehive Lane

I was born in May 1923 in Beehive Lane, Galleywood. The house is still standing, modernized and now named Carlton Cottages, though when I lived there it didn't have a name. My father worked on the Carlton House Estate and we kept poultry and rabbits. I received 6d a week pocket money for helping to look after them.

On June 12th 1948, I got married at Galleywood church. Both my wife Vi and I had been christened there too, and we were

Chelmsford Cathedral.

21

A sewing card.

married by the Revd F.A. Roughton who served that parish from 1921 to 1958. He was followed by the Revd E.C. Lendon who served from 1958 to 1968. I myself am a Church Warden.

David Cook

A Rubber Wringer

In the early days I mostly did my washing on a Monday. I had a gas copper in which I boiled the washing before putting it through a wringer with rubberized rollers; I then hung the washing out on the line. I did my ironing on Tuesday with the heavy flat irons which we heated on the fire. Of course there were no man made fibres then and the clothes took a lot of ironing. White cotton sheets took ages to dry, especially when they were new.

Mollie Smith

Rag Rugs

When the kids went to bed there was no television but we had an old radio on top of the mantle piece. It only had two stations, Home or Light. Bert and I would sit either side of the fire to listen to the radio and make rag rugs. We could buy old flour sacks with red print on them from the baker, you got a lovely sack for twopence. Bert would cut bits of rags that his mother saved for us while I used an old dolly peg that we had split in half and sharpened as a hook. I forced the hook into the canvas to pull the rag through, after a while the continual pressure made my fingers very sore. We stitched it all up but never lined it. They were warm underfoot and took pride of place but when you came to shake it outside the dust was like a very thick fog.

Molly Watson

Champagne Paint

The Cottage in George Street had wood up to waist height with cupboards each side of the fire place, and we had a couple of second-hand chairs. When we first went in we decided to decorate everywhere so we did all the wood in champagne which was the 'in' colour then, and wallpapered the walls. We got a fire going and had just sat down when there was a terrible cracking noise. All the paper had fallen off the walls; we hadn't realized that you had to size the walls before you decorated them. There were plenty of mice there as Mrs Hines opposite would feed the cats outside so they were always full up and wouldn't catch any.

Mary Ellis

Butter and Cheese

On the farm there were two big cow sheds holding forty-two cows so milk was always available but mother didn't use it; she always had our milk delivered as she thought it would be healthier. Sometimes we made our own butter – this was the only time we had it. We left the milk for a couple of days until it turned sour then skimmed the curds from the top. If we didn't use the whey for cooking either cakes or custard we threw it away, while the curds were put in muslin bags and left to drain for about three days, depending on the weather. When it was semi-solid we added a little salt and used it as soft cheese. The rest of the curds were put into a big jam jar with a lid. We would then shake the jar for many hours everyone taking their turn – the result was fresh butter.

Ida Cunningham

Kitchen Bath Geyser

Up till I was four or five I was bathed in a tin bath in front of the range in the scullery. In Moulsham Street it was the same except in the summer we bathed in the light cellar which was not so much of an upheaval. In Coval Lane in 1938 we had a bath with a Geyser over it at the end of the kitchen. The bath was covered by a table top which we used as a working surface, and when we wanted a bath we hooked the table top up. In Hall Street and Moulsham Street we only had gas lamps but in Coval Lane we had electricity.

Phyllis Everett

The Young People's League

I was still in the Land Army when I joined the Cathedral Young People's League, the 'YPL'. We used to go out regularly together in the evenings. I met my husband in the 'YPL' – he was from Tiptree but lived in digs in Chelmsford, and during the war he was in the Royal Engineers and served mostly in India where he received the British Empire Medal.

Mary Woolf

Chelmer Road

I grew up with my mother and older sister in Chelmer Road. The house is now demolished and the area is a retail park; the house was near to where the big B&Q stands. I attended the Moulsham Road school between the ages of eleven and fifteen years. When I got married in May

1963 at the Trinity Road church my future sister-in-law was one bridesmaid and a small cousin the other. We lived with my mum in Chelmer Road for about three years until we were allocated a council house. I never owned a bike but walked or caught the bus everywhere until I passed my driving test. The first car we owned which my husband drove was a red Ford Escort.

Nina Stanford

Opposite Lionmede

My parents were called Edward and Hilda Lynett and I was born in 1921 in the Springfield Road. The house was opposite Lionmede which is now a public park; when I was a child it was just a field where my sister Joan and I used to play. In those days they used to drive cattle down Springfield Road and through the High Street to the market, and we were then taken by our parents to see the animals at the market.

Barbara Rayment

Sat down for the Queen

My sister lived in First Avenue and we always had a big get-together there at Christmas. After washing up we all sat down for the Queen's Speech and then it was time to unwrap our presents. The children managed to wait, of course – they had already had their stockings in the morning. In my younger days I only went to the cinema occasionally.

Gladys Hilliard

1953 Floods

We were living in Coval Lane in 1953 when there were bad floods. I was curious to see how far the water had come up so I walked to the bottom of the road, turned left to continue down Coval Lane and found I was at the edge of the water. Under the viaduct, ducks were swimming where ducks had never swum before. Another time water was running over the bridge in London Road, we couldn't get into the church and among other damaged items was all the Girl Guides' camping equipment which was under water.

Phyllis Everett

Star Terrace

I was born in Baddow Road at No. 6 Star Terrace, just past the Star pub, in 1928. My father came from Hall Street in Chelmsford; his father was the undertaker whose premises were where the Elim church is now. My father worked at Hoffmans and my mother came from Haverhill to work in the factory – that was where she met my father. She lived with an aunt and uncle over Fulcher's the greengrocer in Duke Street. I have one brother who was born in West Avenue. I can remember as a very small child sitting on my mother's bed talking to her, then I was taken downstairs and when I went back up my baby brother was there with my mother and her midwife. We lived in Baddow Road before moving to the new houses in West Avenue, and when I was nine we moved again to the top of Swiss Avenue.

Mary Ellis

Molly Watson's son, Norman.

Fostering Years

We were in Henry Road for twelve to thirteen years and I had stopped working when I had my three children who were all born in St John's Hospital. I stayed at home to look after them and when my youngest was three or four years old we started to foster children. We fostered from the unmarried mothers' home in South Borough Road; at eight days old the babies came to us directly from St John's. We had many sleepless nights but eventually got it down to a fine art. I went to bed and Bernard did the 10 p.m. feed so I could do the 2 a.m. feed. We fostered ten or twelve babies over a two to three year period; we got used to seeing them come and go, although after each one left Bernard and I would have a day out and treat ourselves. The nappy washing was hard work but we had a washing machine with a mangle on top. The nappies and winceyette night-dresses were the worst things to dry. In our house there was always something drying in front of the fire.

Mary Woolf

25

CHAPTER 2
School

Bert Youell with his mother and brother.

Nature Walks

The Sandon Church of England infants' and junior school was next door to the Crown pub; the school had only two rooms. Mrs Philips taught the infants and Miss Stanley the juniors. It had an outside toilet and was close to the church. Although each teacher taught a wide range of ages in their class we all seemed to learn a lot and there was a happy atmosphere in the school. We took part in church activities and had the benefit of nature walks, I enjoyed my time there.

Lynne Harding

All Women Teachers

I was at school during the war; the teachers were all women as the men were in the armed forces. I thought the school seemed very dark and it took me quite a while to get used to it. I don't remember having books –

just a slate board and marker. The teachers, one I think was called Mrs Henstritch, used an easel.

Bert Youell

Chelmsford County High School

I passed the eleven-plus and went to Chelmsford County High School for Girls in Broomfield Road. They had very strict rules about uniform but we found ways to make it look more attractive specially after we left the school gates and were within range of King Edward VI for boys just down the road! The navy berets were the worst! The uniform was bought at Bonds, now Debenhams, in the town and the berets were huge, stiff, navy blue articles with the school badge on the front. We needed to soak them and wash them vigorously until they were smaller and worn looking. Shoes were a problem: they had to be navy or black brogues – very unflattering. The blazer was a thing bought by parents in the first year and rapidly abandoned for a navy cardigan or jumper, a better option. The skirts we hooked up about six or eight inches and the school tie was loosened to hang fetchingly at half mast or removed as soon as possible. In summer we wore blue and white check dresses, white socks and straw boaters which, thank goodness, were optional.

Diane Watson

Brushing for the Shoot

On Sundays I went to the little tin Bethel chapel along Chignal Road. It was over a mile's walk and we would go Sunday morning, again for afternoon Sunday school and again for the evening service. During the week I went to Chignal Church of England School. We walked a mile and a half in all weathers. My first headmistress was Miss Brooks, then later Miss Day came. The infants' teacher was Miss Turner, and the junior teacher was Mrs Beardsmore. The landlord of the Three Elms public house had a son, Geoff Byford, who farmed the land owned by the parish. I would help at harvest time and loved sitting in the combine harvester. Every winter I went 'brushing' for the 'shoot'; the farmer would come to the school and he always asked for me by name as he wanted me to bring along a few mates to go 'brushing', I got half a crown and a brace of rabbits. Every other Saturday I went with Mr Shead and Mr Crawley rabbiting – I got half a crown for that too. I left that school when I was fourteen years old.

Ted Revell

Collision with a Tractor

One foggy day when we were on the bus going home from school a tractor came out of a field near Boreham and knocked the bus into a ditch. The driver got all the children off and told us to wait. A National bus came along and picked the children up, but I decided not to hang around and had already left, taking my sister and marching off into the fog heading for home. We had nearly reached Witham when a police car picked us up. As I was only seven I didn't get into too much trouble.

Pat Gillen

Douglas Catt in 1918.

Cathedral School

My children started at the Cathedral School and my daughter later went to the County High School for Girls, one son went to Broomfield and the other to Patchinghall Lane which was a technical school. One of my sons still lives in Chelmsford; my other children live in Kent and Maldon.

Mary Woolf

Kings Road School

I went to Kings Road School and I still see some of my old Kings Road friends – Pauline Lawrence, Joy Codey, Joyce Hurren, Margaret Warner and Marie Puxley who had a lovely voice. Also Jean Reid who arranges our reunions and Eva Smith. The teachers I remember included Miss Mellar who was headmistress, Miss Wright, Miss Cook and Miss Clay the art teacher. I was thirteen when I left Kings Road to spend a year at Rainsford School and I think Miss Mellar went to Rainsford herself. She was a nice person.

Mary Ellis

Trinity Road School

I went to Trinity Road school and left in 1938. It was a good school for sport and had a good reputation too for children passing the eleven-plus examination. The headmaster was Mr Hutchinson who ruled with a rod of iron. Some of the children came to school with no shoes on in those days. The building looks much the same now as it did then. I had a brother and two sisters; we all went there. I enjoyed those years. We walked the two miles to school and came home at dinner time, too. You could take sandwiches but that meant you had to eat them in the playground whatever the weather.

Pete Huckle

Navy Blue Knickers

We also had to wear navy blue knickers and long socks. In needlework classes the navy blue knickers were one of the first things we had to learn to sew. How I hated the lesson and the knickers; and how scared I was of Miss Weston the teacher! She took needlework and cookery lessons. She terrified us with a look: she didn't have to shout but commanded immediate obedience. Her classes were conducted in petrified silence. I ditched both needlework and cookery as soon as I could. Our needlework necessities we kept in our individual biscuit tins which were stored in a cupboard in the classroom. Mine was painted a very bright pink and was instantly recognizable.

Diane Watson

Miss Gladstone

My first primary school was in the London Road. My uncle, who was married to mother's twin sister, took me to school. I later went to another primary school in Hill Road run by Miss Gladstone. In 1924 my parents had an interview with the headmaster Mr Thomas Hay at the King Edward VI Grammar School. I was accepted into the school and stayed there until 1928 when I was fifteen. The teachers I particularly remember are Mr Finlay, Mr Johnson who we called 'Pussy' Johnson and 'Copper' Smith.

Douglas Catt

Miss Cadbury

Miss Cadbury was headmistress, someone far removed from day-to-day school life and held in awe by us all. I remember she was slim with short, pale hair and quietly spoken. Her office was in the front of the building on the right before the doors to the Assembly Hall. It was

Diane Watson in High School uniform.

rare to find yourself on the chairs outside her room; Miss Weston often dealt with any wrongdoers, she was much more frightening. You would sit, trembling, on chairs outside her small office waiting to be reprimanded mostly for inconsequential misdemeanours like talking in class or daydreaming. I've been guilty of both!

Diane Watson

The Friars School

My first school was 'Friars'. It was an infants' school and stood where Parkway is now – it was only a short walk from where we lived. Miss Golding was headmistress and Mrs Wright the reception teacher. At seven I left infants' school and went to St John's girls' school which was in Moulsham Street next to the church; the building is still there. Miss Kathleen Phillips was headmistress, Miss Skilton my class teacher, and other teachers were called Miss Stark and Miss Firman.

In 1938 at the age of thirteen I passed the thirteen-plus entrance exam to the Mid Essex Technical College which was like a trade school. There I studied commercial subjects until June 1940 when, because I had a job to go to, I was allowed to leave three weeks before the end of term. I left college Friday and started work at Marconi's as a shorthand typist/clerk on the following Monday. I stayed at Marconi's for forty-five years, moving around the different departments in their offices.

Between 1939 and 1940 things had changed and I studied part-time. Evacuated schools from London came down to share our classrooms and we were divided into morning and afternoon shifts. This only lasted for a few weeks as Chelmsford was not a safe place either.

Phyllis Everett

Miss Wright

There was Miss Wright who took music. One lesson was devoted to appreciation of classical music and we would listen to gramophone records of famous symphonies. Miss McKenna taught geography. Miss Blacker took games, as also did Miss Hunter who played hockey for Essex and England, I believe. We were taught tennis; I played for the school team one year and we were against Ilford who fielded Christine Truman in their team. In summer we also played cricket. This was obligatory and the hard leather ball frequently connected to ankles and shins. We conspired all manner of medical excuses to avoid cricket. We had a sports day each year when parents were invited.

Diane Watson

Canon Paynter

I went to the High School aged eleven years. My mother wanted me to go but my father felt women didn't need educating. I cycled to school on a bike that Canon Paynter had bought for me. I had that bike for years. I would cycle up Victoria Road and Rectory Lane and at lunch time I would cycle all the way home and back to school again. I saw the Hoffman workers all cycling home when they finished at 12.30 after the morning shift. The head teacher was called Miss Bancroft. She was quite an old lady when she retired and I think she was very good. I was in Tancock House but there was also Pennyfeather and Chancellor. I left when I was seventeen with my Cambridge certificate.

Ivy Holden

The Death of Gandhi

At school I remember the class being told about the death of Gandhi. It was the first time we were taught about an international leader and the teacher explained about nationalism and Gandhi's policy of passive resistance to us. I have always remembered that lesson and been very impressed with what a great man he was.

Pat Gillen

Perils of Drinking

Miss Jackson took biology, a tall lady with long, white hair in a bun. She was fair-skinned and blushed easily especially when introducing us to human reproduction and the perils of drinking, poor woman. Miss Sharples was science mistress. The labs were behind the main building and looked across the playing fields, which was fatal if what was going on outside was more interesting than what went on inside. Miss Winter was art mistress; I spent a lot of time in the art room and was greatly encouraged by her. But most inspiring was the history teacher Miss Johnson, who taught with a passion and made the subject come alive. She had a pet phrase 'it all boils down to', which she repeated constantly. The Latin mistress was a dear lady who tried to teach a difficult subject and was often diverted away from declensions and vocabulary by ingenious girls. Miss Owers taught us scripture or religious instruction as they call it now – she was a very devout woman. For English we learnt long pieces of poetry and prose by heart and always had to read aloud.

Diane Watson

Blots on New Books

I remember we had new books at the Springfield School and were told not to get blots on them. I did, of course, and got rapped across the hand for that. We had a playing field and toilets out back near the railway line and we would stand on the fence and watch the trains go by. A nurse would come to look through our hair for nits; she came regularly and we stood with our hands behind our backs as she looked at our hair. Later we called her 'Nitty Nora', but not until later.

Ivy Holden

Dancing Round the Maypole

When I was five I started at Trinity Road infants' school; my sister was already there. I remember Miss Jenkins, who was very straight laced and strict; also I remember watching an air ship through the school windows. On Empire Day we would wave flags and on May Day we enjoyed dancing round the maypole. I left school when I was fifteen years old, then went to a Business Training School in Chelmsford where I learned shorthand and typing.

Barbara Rayment

Best Friends

I was Diane Smith when I was at school. My best friends all through school years at the County High were Rosemary Peacock, Jennifer Mussell and Valerie Dines. But I counted the whole class as friends and remember them all now: Barbara Gibbard, Pat Mead, Barbara Bassett, Gillian Rice, Anne Woolf, Jennifer Woodrow, Susan Rolfe, Susan Lee, Ann Phipps, Carol Sheffield, Ann Pearce, Stella Brinson, Celia Lowe, Judith Pond, Valerie Fenton,

31

Classmates at the High School.

Maureen Ward, Mary Wells, Janet Hull, Valerie Clark, Valerie Cooper, Margaret Burgess, Frances Mansfield, Linda Westrip, Valerie Moss, Susan Mills, Delia Headford, Jackie Hammond, Michele Fedida, Margarita Gillam, Joan Groves, Olive Ridgewell. I think I've remembered most of them.

Diane Watson

Cap and Gown

When I started Secondary school at Sandon the headmaster was Mr Harvey. He was an exceptional teacher for that time: he didn't believe in corporal punishment and always wore his cap and gown. There were lessons in French and German, the sciences included chemistry, physics and biology, though the girls still did cookery and the boys woodwork. Every Friday we had form meetings where we elected a chairperson and spokesman. If there were any complaints we elected someone to follow it through and report back with the results. I was once elected to challenge a teacher who was accused of bullying one of the boys. The teacher was mortified but her attitude towards the boy improved. I had every opportunity offered to me by that school – lots of people took advantage of it and went on to do very well.

Lynne Harding

Cold Rice

I went to school at St Philip's Priory in London Road. My brother, sister and I would cycle every day from Writtle. We wore a brown and gold uniform, a brown gymslip and shantung blouse with a little brown felt hat. The head of the convent was the Mother Prioress; we had a Mother Prioress feast day in the middle of summer and my father made up a bouquet of sweet peas and I gave them to Mother Prioress. Sister Loyola taught us French. If she was cross she threw the book at us: she had a very short fuse. Mind you we did take the mickey, but they were very strict there. On Friday we always had fish and with the fish we had boiled rice. I could not stand boiled rice but if you didn't eat it you had to stay at the table. They would say, 'Some little black babies would love that rice.' I would say in my heart 'They can have it,' but I had to eat it. If I felt sick or if it was cold, my brother would be laughing at me across the table, as in those days it was a sin not to eat your dinner. I stayed at that school until I was sixteen when I got my Cambridge Certificate and left.

Mary Woolf

Miss Waddley

My sisters and I went to Kings Road Infants' School. We walked the few yards from our home. Miss Waddley was headmistress. We then went on to the junior school where Miss Mellor was headmistress and some of the other teachers were Miss Kelly, Miss Armstrong and a Miss Pretty. My class friends were Olive Crosier and Kathy Charlton. We didn't wear a uniform and we all went home for our lunch. My children also went to Kings Road School, later going on to Rainsford School. They both married and are settled in Chelmsford.

Gladys Hilliard

Saints' Days

I went to Springfield Church of England Primary School and on any of the Saints' Days we would march across Springfield Green to the church service in the morning then have the rest of the day off. I left school when I was fourteen years old.

Sally Pattendon

Sisters of Mercy

I was taught by the Sisters of Mercy at the Church of Our Lady Immaculate school in London Road; the school was at the back of the church. It was a small school with mixed-sex classes and about one hundred pupils. It was a non-paying Catholic school and we did not wear a uniform, but the nuns were very strict. We went there until we were fifteen. We had school lunches – they were tasty and cost a couple of shillings a week. The pupils who attended the Priory, just up the road, were taught by the same Nuns as us; they did wear a uniform and the Priory was a fee paying school.

Pat Gillen

A Joint Social Evening

In the breaks and lunch hour, if it was wet, we would play jacks on the classroom floor or hangman on the blackboard. But unless it rained cats and dogs or the snow was deep we would have to be outside in the playing fields.

I recall we once had a joint social evening at King Edward VI School, probably in the fifth form, when we were invited to a dance. It was a very uncomfortable evening with boys on one side and the girls on the other and also some teachers were present. Very formal, different to the discos they enjoy today. Apart from that once which I think may have been an experiment, we were not encouraged to fraternize with the boys which, of course, made them seem more interesting.

Diane Watson

Miss Philips and Miss Ferman

I went to St John's School in Moulsham Street. When I was five they were going to build a school in Lady Lane. The council bought a field which was called Hayfield; it was a place we all played in as kids. They didn't develop it but instead they built Moulsham School at a much later date; consequently I spent all my school years at St John's School. The headmistress of the Junior and Senior Schools was Miss Philips who lived up Vicarage Road. I liked Miss Ferman, she was the dancing teacher and we went to all the folk dances and to the contests against other schools which was held on the old football ground in New Writtle Street. The whole field would be filled with children from all the other schools. Miss Ferman lived in Roman Road. I learnt knitting from school and have continued to do it ever since. I also went to Sunday School at St John's; the morning classes were held at the Parish Hall, Vicarage Road.

Doris Wesley

Mr Coward

I went to the little church school near Springfield Green, which has since been pulled down. The Springfield School headmaster was called Mr Coward; there was a Miss Cutts and another teacher, whose name I can't recall, who rode to school on her bike with her umbrella up. There were about one hundred pupils at the school and I was the first child to win a scholarship to the High School.

Ivy Holden

Waterloo Lane Nursery

My two eldest boys went to the Waterloo Lane nursery while I was at work. They have now turned part of this building into a restaurant. It cost 2s 6d a day for each child and that included breakfast and a mid-day meal. The nursery took young babies to school-age children and it was run by a matron, sister and qualified nursery nurses. The children were also bathed and had a change of clothes daily. I picked them up at 4.30 p.m. and took them home; they only needed their faces washing and something more to eat before going to bed.

Molly Watson

Rainsford School

I went to Kings Road infants' and junior school. Dr Moon was the headmaster and other teachers I remember were Mrs Higgins, Mrs Taylor and Mr Billington, who was the music teacher. I left Kings Road when I was eleven years old in 1949

Corporation Road Nursery School.

and went to Rainsford School. Mr G. Cock was headmaster and other teachers were Mr Morgan, Mrs Morgan, Mr Woodcroft, Mr Wiffen, Mr Richards the art teacher, Mr Winter and Mr Upson. I wore a black school blazer with a badge.

George Christodoulou

Edward VI's Grammar

In 1930/31 my brother Ron went to Edward VI's Grammar School. He was the only one of us who went there; the rest of us, although near the top of our classes, went to Great Baddow School until we were fourteen years old. The family could not afford to send more than one child to the grammar school. Ron biked to school and after leaving he got a job in County Hall.

Ida Cunningham

School Dinners

We all stayed for school dinners – no one brought sandwiches or left the school premises in the lunch hour. We lined up and went into the dining hall, where long tables were laid end to end with a prefect at the head and those on the end of the benches were servers who collected the meals from the kitchen. The prefects dished up from the metal containers. I remember some poor girls still there when the rest had left because they hadn't finished everything up.

There was what we called 'stodge', a sponge type pudding sometimes with jam or treacle. Lots of stews and vegetables, rarely chips but occasionally something good like chocolate pudding with chocolate sauce. Much semolina, tapioca and rice pudding for desserts. A treat would be shortbread.

Diane Watson

Galleywood Village School

I went to Galleywood village school which is now a youth centre. The headmaster was Mr J.W. Smith who was a schoolmaster of the 'old school' – he waved and used his cane regularly. There were several nice lady teachers; I remember particularly Miss Rowland and Miss Cook. When I was thirteen I and another lad were the first two to pass the entrance exam for the Mid Essex Technical College junior section to take a three-year engineering course. I then went on to the senior section day release. I had my first bike when I went to the Technical College so I could cycle there and back. I did the engineering and my friend the commerce course; there was also an arts course and among other things I studied drawing, metalwork and a lot of maths which I enjoyed.

David Cook

George with his father, foster mother and brother John.

The End of Peace

We had the first year in peacetime, until mid-1939. We were told at the beginning of the summer holidays: 'If war breaks out don't come back, wait to hear what to do.' We didn't rejoin on the September date and we were told to report to the school playing fields at the top of North Avenue. A master met us and gave us work to do – eventually we did go back.

Phyllis Everett

CHAPTER 3
Work

An Austin towing vehicle as portrayed on a Christmas card.

Messenger Boy

I left school and went to my first job at Eastern National buses in the timetables office. I spent all the working hours reading out the timetables to the senior clerk. It drove me up the wall. Then when I was fifteen years I went to Marconi's and then in January 1940 I joined the Fire Service as a part time messenger boy. As a messenger boy I attended all fires on my motorbike; in those days there were no phones or radio links, only three alarm positions in Chelmsford, so I would take messages to and fro on my motorbike.

Pete Huckle

£5 5s for a Sixty-Hour Week

I was the first man in Essex to have changed from a part-time fireman to a full-time one. I joined the National Fire Service when I was seventeen and a half in June 1944 as a part timer. I received a small retaining fee and expenses and was stationed at the fire station in Dunmow. I transferred to Chelmsford as a full-timer on the 30 December 1948 with a wage of £5 5s for a sixty-hour week. I was sent on a training course to Dagenham, which was still part of Essex in those days. The course lasted for twelve weeks and on completion we had a passing out parade. The service was transferred back to the county of Essex on the 1st April 1948.

Dave Wright

Scoffield and Martin

When I left school I started work at my father's shop. He had arranged to send me to Southend to Scoffield and Martin, a chain of grocery shops, where I could gain experience in the trade. Scoffield of Scoffield and Martin was Mayor of Southend. When the year ended I went back to my father's shop where I worked until the Second World War started.

Douglas Catt

The GPO

When I started work at the telephone exchange in Chelmsford my wages were £4 10s a week. There were a lot of people working there, with about thirty-five boards and each board had approximately fifty connections. I first of all went to Norwich on a six-week training course; the GPO paid our expenses, lodgings and food. There were half a dozen supervisors who earned at least 20s a week more and who we referred respectfully to as Mrs 'Whatever' – never by their Christian names. The daytime shift were always female, with some males working the night shift. The exchange was situated in Cottage Place, behind the Cathedral.

Maureen Wiseman

15s a Week

When I first started work at Marconi's, I earned 15s a week, but after a few weeks I got a birthday rise and it went up to £1. We had birthday rises up to a certain age, after which the rises were on merit. Initially I went home for lunch but after a while I ate in the canteen.

Phyllis Everett

Hessian Grub Bag

When harvesting was being done in the middle of the day we used to take my father his hessian grub bag filled with chunks of bread, sometimes cheese or meat, and his tea in a big enamel can with a handle at the side and a cup on top. The bread would be wrapped in greaseproof paper.

Ida Cunningham

Dupex Lamps

I left school when I was fourteen and went to work at Grippers in the High Street where

George Christodoulou of the Rainsford Youth Committee.

Halfords were. They were ironmongers and I went as an assistant. For the first six months, my job each morning was to get on a ladder and dust the dupex lamps that hung from the wooden ceiling and had wide tin shades. I only had Wednesday afternoons off and earned 12s 6d a week. I stayed there fourteen years off and on.

Mary Ellis

Mess Manager

In 1948 there were about five or six of us on each shift at the fire station. We had the use of a dormitory when we were on night duty and there was also a rest room, dining room and of course a kitchen. The brigade employed a cook during the day but we took it in turns to cook when we were on the late shift. I had a spell as Mess Manager: this entailed deciding on the menu and actually

going to the shops and buying the provisions. Food was still rationed until 1951, but firemen were a necessary service and we all received a special allowance – after all a hungry fireman might not be very effective. The men paid for their food on a weekly basis – it was always a set charge as Mess Managers worked within a budget.

Dave Wright

Weekend Waiter

My natural father who ran a restaurant in London visited us once a year. When I was sixteen I did some waitering in his restaurant. I would leave home at 6 p.m. Saturday evening and go by train to Paddington, work in his restaurant and come back Sunday night.

George Christodoulou

ENO Company

I worked for the Eastern National Omnibus Company in the 1960s. I worked in the accounts department and my duties were to calculate the log sheets and make sure that the bus tickets sold agreed with the money collected. My hours were between 9 a.m. and 5 p.m. There were nine of us in the office with a manager and three overseers. It was a big, airy room with plenty of space for everyone; you can still see it from the outside of the building as you walk by. My friends in the office were Pat Butler and Gwen Wyebrow. Gwen worked in the lost property department. Of course we all got free bus travel and subsidized meals in the canteen. The meals were exceptionally good and the canteen was well used by staff, drivers and conductors. I learnt a lot from the bus company including how to use a Comptometer machine and it was where I first became interested in being a telephonist.

Margaret Brannan

Widford Golf Course

I stayed two years in Chelmsford between 1926 and 1928, doing odd jobs, mainly caddying on the Widford Golf Course. I charged 2s 6d for a round and usually was hired for two rounds a day. I was given an extra tanner [sixpence] for a drink. I was in demand as I had a knack for advising them on the weather conditions and also I was one of the first to clean the irons with a rag after use. I lived in a row of very old shiplap timber houses which were pulled down after the war even though there was nothing wrong with them. I lodged with

Margaret Brannan and Pat Butler.

my elder sister in Widford village and gave her some of my wages for my keep. One of my sisters married into the Brazier family and one into the Dawsons. I believe their children and grandchildren are still in Chelmsford to this day. I liked a drink and often spent time in the Evelyn Woods and the White Horse at Widford.

Bill Woolley

Springfield Road

After the war Bert got a job as a caretaker at a 'workers' hostel'. I did the cooking and housekeeping with a young girl helper. The hostel was in Springfield Road and the building is now used by the Public Health Office. Springfield Road was different then: next door we had a doctor and a dentist and opposite were two grocery shops which are no longer there. While we were working and living at the hostel a new hotel was built, two hairdressers opened and the road began to get commercial.

Molly Watson

120 Men from Wales

The fire brigade is a very close knit community. Sometimes two or three days might go by without the shift being called out to a fire, and during the waiting time there was a lot of opportunity to talk with the other men and we really got to know each other well. There were a limited amount of leisure facilities available but after working closely with the same people for many years its almost like being part of a family. 1953 was the year of the East Coast Floods. It was so severe that, as well as the Essex Brigade, we were sent 120 men from Wales. We all worked together along the coastline round Burnham-on-Crouch, pumping the water back into the sea. A few years later in 1958 there was a tremendous thunderstorm one Friday night and it poured with rain for over a week. Chelmsford was completely flooded and we were really busy. One of the last places to be pumped out was the football ground in Writtle Street. On the whole I would say that extremes of weather, either hot or cold, were our busiest times.

Dave Wright

Marconi Marine

When I was fourteen I got a job at Driver's Printers in Tindal Street as an apprentice. When I started I earnt 7s a week and after six months it went up to 15s. Out of my 7s I would give my mother 5s and kept 2s for myself. I smoked a bit: I remember cigarettes were 6d for a packet of ten John Players. I was at Driver's a couple of years when we moved to Corporation Road opposite the County High School. When I left I went to work at Simmonds Printers in Baddow Road but then the war broke out and the print trade went bust. I went to Marconi's and started work as a messenger, moving later to the accounts department of Marconi Marine in New Street. I was called up in 1942 and spent 4_ years in the Army. I met my wife in Shropshire and we married in 1944; my wife also found work at Marconi's.

Ted Revell

Edna Duffield's Florist

When I was fourteen years old I left school and then went down to the Labour Exchange to see what jobs were going. They offered me a job as a junior at Edna Duffield's florists in London Road. I was paid 5s a week and they trained me to make wreaths, bouquets and all the other normal floristry tasks. I stayed there until I was eighteen when I left to work at Marconi's, though I did return to the florists briefly and worked part-time hours after I was married and had my children. I worked at Marconi's in New Street and I was set to sorting out components for transmitters. The manager was called Mr Woods and his second in charge was called Mr Bowler. I didn't earn a lot of money but stayed there for either four or five years before leaving to get married.

Gladys Hilliard

Ted Revell aged sixteen years.

Nursemaid at Broomfield

I had always been interested in caring for children so when I left school at fourteen I took a job as nursemaid to a family at Broomfield. They lived in 'Southwinds', a big house in Patching Hall Lane; it stood right back with a long, sloping drive. I had to look after a little girl of two; her father Mr Pearce worked for Cockburn Port in London and travelled up by train each day. Mrs Pearce who was the daughter of Ripon the newsagent helped her mother in their business. I looked after Valerie at home and was treated as one of the family. I took Valerie for long walks in the Tansad pushchair round the lanes in Broomfield and Chelmsford, I did the odd bit of shopping and helped with the housework though there was a char lady for the main cleaning.

Ida Cunningham

Bond's Shoe Department

When I left school my father, who worked for Lord Rayleigh then, told me to go to Bond's (a posh store, a sort of local Harrods), and ask for a job. I was lucky and they employed me in the children's section of their shoe department. I was then sent to the Clark's training school in Somerset for one week where we learnt the correct method of measuring people's feet. I started

Clark's factory in Somerset.

off at £2 7s 6d a week and always had to wear black shoes with a black skirt and white blouse. Of course, I could not afford to buy my shoes from Bonds so had to buy them at a cheaper shop. The hours were 9 a.m. to 5.30 p.m. and we were required to sign in a book that was placed in each department on arrival.

Mr Desborough was in charge: he was very strict but fair. There were five of us in my section, Linda Guymer who was also fifteen years old, two older girls Shirley and Jenny who were at least twenty and Mrs Simmons who was second in charge to Mr Desborough.

As long as we did our work we could have a laugh and chat and I enjoyed working there. Bonds had their own canteen where we could have a packed lunch or buy cooked food at a much cheaper price.

I only got into trouble once and that was when I was in charge of the children's section. This posh lady and her children came in at nearly 5.30 p.m. and I had to get a lot of shoes out for them to try on. Linda came up and said it was time to go and I replied, 'I can't, that — woman is still asking for shoes.' Unfortunately the customer overheard and reported me. The next day I was called to the office but as the remark had been made after 5.30 p.m. and my only bus home left at 5.45 p.m. they understood and let me off with a warning.

Maureen Wiseman

River of Suet

At Hoffmans at lunchtime we would take our packed lunch to the café next to Newcomes Garage where we could buy a cup of tea and eat our lunch. The proprietor and his wife ran the café; he was called Stan. Afterwards we stood outside and talked about sport before going back to the factory. Opposite the works was a newsagents and sweet shop, two mobile vans sold papers outside and on Fridays we would see cattle or sheep driven down Rectory Lane and New Street on their way to market. Opposite Marconi's was a railway goods yard where animals coming to market were unloaded and near the railway bridge was the Atora Suet factory which was bombed during the war and the suet melted and ran down the road.

Dennis Smith

Messenger and Call Boy

I lived in Threadneedle Street with my parents and twin sisters. My father had joined the fire brigade in 1918 and I was employed by them when I was fifteen and a

Bond's in Chelmsford.

Red Watch with the Pump Competition cup.

half in 1935. It was Chelmsford Borough Fire Brigade then and I was the messenger and call boy to the Chief Officer. I ran various errands for him but one duty I had to carry out every day was to test the three street fire alarms. They consisted of a pole with a glass section on the top, and it was wired up somehow so that in the case of a fire the glass could be broken enabling the person to contact the station directly. One was positioned in Kings Road, a second in Widford Road and the third one I had to cycle to in Springfield. These posts were gradually phased out as telephones became more popular in the mid-50s. Over the years the authorities in charge of the brigade changed from Chelmsford Borough to the Auxialiary FB, then with the onset

of war to the National FB and finally to Essex County FB.

Harold Wakelin

Diesel Fuel Pumps

In 1952 at the end of my engagement in the RAF I decided not to sign up again and came back to Chelmsford. We had two rooms and a shared kitchen in a house in Wallace Crescent which we shared with an old timer from World War One who had been shell-shocked. I then got a job in the workshops of Eastern National Bus Company working on diesel pumps. I was there for ten months and joined the fire

Albert Watson in uniform.

service in May 1953. There were a lot of ex-servicemen in the service so it felt like home from home.

Doug Pheasant

Workers Hostel

The workmen at the hostel who were building Melbourne Park Estate (which until then had been open fields) mostly came from Devon or London. It was a very long day – we started work at 6 a.m. and didn't finish until 10.30 p.m. Our joint wage was £7 a week but we lived rent free and the electric and gas was paid for. The girl

worked from 10 a.m. to 5 p.m. and earned 10s a week, which was good money then. There was a gas cooker and a wooden stove and we provided a cooked breakfast, packed lunch and an evening meal for fifteen men and cleaned their rooms every day. Bert was in charge of the business side and maintenance. The men paid 27s a week to the council and Bert collected the money and looked after any complaints; he also held the men's ration books. I phoned the order through and groceries would be delivered from Perks near the Cathedral; it is I believe a wine bar today. The stuff was still on ration – the shopkeeper would put things aside for regular customers and always let us know when they were expecting a special delivery. I would order very large tins of whole, red tomatoes; they tasted lovely and cost 1s 6d each. I would buy two tins for breakfast. Eggs were one penny each and best back bacon 1s 6d a pound with streaky at 11½d. The sides of bacon were hung in the shop and sliced to order; most people liked the fat on rashers as you could fry bread in it. At 10.30 p.m. we would prepare and pack the lunches for the next day. We used eight loaves; the sandwiches were wrapped in greaseproof paper then put into blue or brown sugar bags before being put in a tray on the counter, each man picking one up on his way to work. The evening meal was usually either shepherd's pie, Cornish pasties or stews. The pies and pasties were made with corned beef, onions and potatoes, as beef was impossible to get. The corned beef was purchased in big long tins for 4s. From the pork butcher we bought twopenn'orth of bones and added pearl barley, turnips and other vegetables. I cooked the stew in an iron cauldron, the bones were meaty and nice and juicy to suck, full of goodness. If you had rabbit, it

Molly Watson at English Electric.

was party time! We always had either rice pudding or treacle pudding with custard, I mean real custard. On holidays I cooked either apple or rhubarb pie. Some of the men were married and went home at weekends from Friday evening to Sunday evening. They always took their washing home and the single ones did their own.

Molly Watson

Firewomen

I started work at Chelmsford fire station when I was nineteen years old in 1965. I was employed as a firewoman though firewomen never went out to the fires – we were trained to be in charge of the control room. There were always two of us in the control room: a Senior Leading Officer and someone of a junior rank, and if either of these women were unable to turn up for duty a fireman that they had previously trained stood in for them. The consul was in the centre of the room and a map of the area hung on the wall, it was a very responsible job as Chelmsford at that time was the Divisional Control and covered a large area from Ingatestone, Maldon, Witham round to Great Waltham. Firewomen were not paid as much as the men though they came under the same discipline. We were always treated with a great deal of respect, brought cups of tea, they were a smashing bunch to work with.

Lynne Harding

Model Laundry

After the war I went back briefly to Marconi's. My wife also found work at

Ted Revell at Hoffmans.

Marconi's. I left there and drove a laundry delivery van for Chelmsford Model Laundry in Victoria Road where the police station is now. I was there three years and then got a job as an adult apprentice at Hoffmans in their tool department. I stayed there almost until the factory's closure.

Ted Revell

5s a Week Extra

After the war I'd decided not to go back to the fire service as it was not well paid. I went to see the lads at the station which was where the 'Oasis' is now – it had moved from the town due to the bombing. The whole complex contained eight bays and a control room etc. It was there from about 1942/1943

Ted and Thelma Huckle with Australian friends.

The Hoffman works.

to July 1959 when it moved to its present location. The Divisional Officer said if I came back without taking another job meantime I would get 5s a week extra for every year done in the Army. So I had seven years and it would be 35s on top, so it was then £4 10s a week. After six months I would then be able to pay my back pension – they would take £1 5s out of my wages. I rejoined in 1947 and was thirty-four years in total in the service. I came out in 1974 when I was fifty years old. I loved every minute of the life; I felt I was helping someone every day, but it was important to mix well and have an understanding wife.

Pete Huckle

The Jig and Tool Department

I was born in 1919 and raised in Kelvedon. When I went to Colchester Technical School I played football against Chelmsford Technical School and cricket against Chelmsford Grammar School, but apart from that Chelmsford was a closed book until I came to work here in 1936. I left school at sixteen and my old infants teacher said to my father, 'I can get him a job.' Her brother was Chief Cashier at the old Hoffman Company. I had my interview with Mr Hymas, the manager of J Department, so I came as an apprentice in the Jig and Tool Department, or J Department as it was called. The department was responsible for making the tooling for the manufacture of ball bearings; where I worked is now a two-bedroomed apartment in Durrant Court.

Dennis Smith

War Declared

In 1939 at the end of August we went to Little Clacton for a short holiday. Mr Pearce had rented a bungalow, it was very old and I can still recall the dark wallpaper. Stuffed reptiles were hanging in the hall and they made us shudder. We went to the beach often and Valerie loved it – we were all happy. We were on the beach when war was declared. Mr Pearce, an officer in the Reserves, had taken his radio with us as he was very worried about the political situation. Mrs Pearce drove him home in their Morris 10 then returned to finish the holiday with us. We had been happy: the day before, we had collected oysters. It was the first time I'd tasted them but of course the shine had gone of the holiday and we returned home.

Ida Cunningham

Red Watch with cup. From the left: Peter Newton, Doug Pheasant, Tony Creek, Don Hedgecock and Ivor Parker.

Designed by Chelmsford Men

In 1965 the fire engines were a pump, a pump escape and also a third one called the retained pump. The retained pump was used by firemen who had regular jobs but would respond to either the bell in their house or the big siren on City Hall; this was the siren that had been used as a warning all through the war and is now used to warn of flood dangers. The men from the Chelmsford brigade made a unique contribution to the fire service by designing and developing a hose-laying lorry and a bridging unit that fitted inside the lorry; this enabled hoses to be arched from a distance even across a road. It was in service in Chelmsford for a long while but owing to man shortage is now used by another station. The men and women at the station played volleyball and pool during some of their breaks.

Lynne Harding

Tortoise Stoves

After my training at Dagenham in 1953 I was sent to Chelmsford station which was where the Oasis is now. The huts we were in were so old that when there was a storm the roof would lift and snow came in. We had old Tortoise stoves for heating and the fumes were enough to kill you if the wind was in the wrong direction. Those nearer the stove were lucky but those in the far corners were not so well off. We slept in metal bedsteads. We moved to our present site in 1959. The first pole I saw was at the new place in Waterhouse Lane. It could be hazardous if you were not quick off the bottom, as you got kicked in the ear by the next one down. They had central heating but more polishing because of the tiled floors – also the appliance bays were all tiles. We did all the cleaning then. Slowly brass was going out and chrome was coming in and there is no cleaning by the men any more.

Doug Pheasant

Quartz Crystals

I went to Marconi's where I worked with quartz crystal; my husband was employed in the test room. We married in 1940. My husband was in the Merchant Navy during the war and I made our home in Great Baddow. After the war we bought a house in Broomfield Road and remained there for the next nineteen years.

Sally Pattendon

Working Rotas

When I started back in the fire service we were on a seventy-two-hour week but later we did a sixty-hour week which continued right up to 1974. After that it was forty-eight hours and now its a forty-two hour rota. There was one week of days and one week of nights, and on Sundays the duty was from 10 a.m. until 9 a.m. the next morning. My wife Thelma often spent the day with other firemen's wives. My night shift was 6 p.m. to 9 a.m. next morning; if my children wanted to tell me something they would leave notes. If firemen worked a twenty-four-hour shift the county would have to pay subsistence so we were allowed to work twenty-three hours. During the war at first we did forty-eight hours on and twenty-four hours off, all the time, with no

let up at all. We were given a P24 which gave us an extra day off, just before I joined the Forces.

Pete Huckle

Peters & Barham

After I worked at the GPO as a telephonist I went to Peters & Barham, the ready mixed concrete company, because the hours were more suitable than the nine to five split shifts of the GPO. Also Peters & Barham offered me more money than I had been earning. I was lucky as their first choice for the job failed to turn up and I had a second chance.

Thirty iron steps led up to the office at the back of the Co-op; their storage depot was elsewhere. My duties included taking orders over the phone from the customers who paid for the goods COD. It was really nice to work there with David Holmes and someone called Jack. I was there for about three years; all the girls were friendly and came to my wedding. One of them was a Dutch lady from Broomfield Road – her name was Alida Lumb.

Margaret Brannan

Manual Book-keeping

When I started work in the Accounts Department in the late '50s all the accounts entries had to be entered by hand. The ledgers were massive and extremely heavy and we had to cross check all our work every day. We were forbidden to use a pencil as all entries had to remain; if we had made a mistake we had to clearly show

Mollie Smith as a young woman.

the alteration and sign our names by it. We used blue and red ink and the firm's auditors used green when they did their quarterly checks. The chief auditors were formidable and we had to account for everything we did, but their articled clerks were young like us and we all liked their visits.

Mary Scott

North Avenue

After we left the hostel the council gave us our first house. The rent was 15s 6d a week but we had a terrible shock when after a

couple of months they raised it to 17s. When Bert got his wages I put the rent in an old tea caddy on the mantle-piece and then said, 'Now, that's the roof over our heads.' The house was in North Avenue and had three bedrooms. My husband Bert started work at the prison as a warder, but he didn't like it – the hours were too long and it was shift work. He wanted to be at home on Sunday to play with the children, so he left.

Molly Watson

Dinner Lady

We had two children: one went to the technical school and the other to Moulsham school. We lived mostly on the Westlands Estate when they were young. When my son started at Moulsham school I took a job as a dinner lady and later became an assistant cook. We prepared meals from scratch and the washing up was done by hand – it was hard work but fun and I had all the school holidays off. I finally went as a cook to the Girls' High School.

Mollie Smith

Hook Ladder Drills

When I started work firemen were still doing hook ladder drills. They would scale the front of the building, pull up the ladder, hook it over the next floor and scale up to the next storey. As you can imagine there were some ghastly accidents, with just a sheer drop if anyone fell. They finally banned hook ladder drills in the '70s. The watch also practised with their breathing apparatus. With a pair of blacked out goggles, something similar to a peg over their nose and a tube from the cylinder on their back in their mouths, they crawled around on the floor trying to find their way out of the room. It was quite a sight to behold and as long as a bell didn't ring we remained both silent and still. The women were taught on site, attending a passing-out parade when our training was finished. The men were really supportive and the first time I had to operate the Call Out the entire Watch came in to make sure I did it right.

Lynne Harding

Farm Handyman

My father worked as a handyman on eight farms. He was also village barber, chimney sweep and thatcher. He learnt his trades from his father who originally came from Great Maplestead. Father travelled round the farms on a little green bike; he carried his tool bag on the handlebars with the longer implements tied to the crossbar, and he also had another bag on his back. He was very short, under five foot, and his boots were size 3. Luckily they made hobnailed boots for boys or he'd have been lost!

Father earned 10s a week and the house was free. He mended fences, built haystacks and did all the handyman jobs on the farms. The threshing tackle came each year and he worked on that for a few days, and there was also several cottages to be thatched and he would use straw from the fields for that. Father wore breeches and puttees which consisted of webbing wound round from ankle to knee so that when harvesting, mice and other wildlife could not run up his trouser legs.

Brass bicycle lamp.

Ida Cunningham

Tube Exchange

I left school in 1938 when I was fourteen years old and I went to Hoffmans. In those days you had to start at the bottom: my first job was to clean the brass at the front door. Although that building is now used as apartments, the brass is still there and every time I walk past I think of how I used to polish it. I spent a few months on the tube exchange – this was a system whereby letters moved throughout the factory. I was then transferred to the Sales Department. I did the filing for a couple of years then became a secretary: before I left school I went to shorthand classes and my father also helped me with shorthand. He had learnt it at the Grammar School so he bought all the books and helped me at home.

Doris Wesley

Pensions

In the Fire Service we had two weeks' holiday in summer. It was to be taken from May to September, and every year it went forward six weeks. We had one week in winter, always between October-November and January-February, we always had paid holidays. We paid 6_ per cent and later 11 per cent towards a pension; it was a lot of money when we were young and bringing up kids but it resulted in a good pension eventually. During the war only the police force, fire brigade and prison officers had pension schemes.

Pete Huckle

Comptometer Operator

When I left the High School at seventeen my father was not keen on me pursuing a career of my choice and he got me a job as a Comptometer Operator at Hoffmans. It was 1934 and I got paid 17s 6d a week.

Ivy Holden

Carlton House Estate

My father worked on the Carlton House Estate earning between 30s and £2 a week. The estate belonged to John Henry Keene who died in the early '30s as a millionaire. His wife who inherited his estate was a great benefactor in the area: she built the Keene Homes in Broomfield Road and the Keene Hall in Galleywood as well as contributing to many other good causes. My father first worked for John Henry Keene as a gardener and we lived in a tied cottage. The estate was sold in 1948 and my father remained with the new owner.

David Cook

Gold Watch

Bert went to Marconi's after he left the prison service. He started at £12 with overtime and Saturday morning paying extra. He was there for forty-two years and received a gold watch on retirement. Workers couldn't afford cars and they would cycle to Marconi's in New street and Hoffman's in Rectory Lane. They went on cycles and they rode side by side down Rectory Lane, turned into Corporation and up Broomfield, and away into the new Melbourne estate where the majority of the workers came from. Then you would see the same thing happen in the evening at six o'clock. The wives would go off on bicycles – they couldn't work during the day because of their families – so as the husbands came in the wives went out. There would be a huge array of different coloured headscarves as they cycled to the factory for the 6 p.m. to 10 p.m. shift.

Molly Watson

The Smell and the Noise

I began my apprenticeship in April 1936 and I remember being picked up from the main Hoffmans gate by another apprentice and taken to the department. It was strange – I had never been in a factory or seen one before and the first thing that hit me was the smell and the noise: with all the machines running the din was terrific. As I walked up

Two pay slips from 1952 and 1960.

the yard out from a door came a chap who I had been to school with. His name was Eric Snowden and he had started the week before me; he has been my life long friend. It was a four-year apprenticeship and I had done three years and six months when the war started.

Dennis Smith

Village Barber

As the village barber my father would set up shop outside the farmhouse in the yard at the back. His customers would sit on the chair to have their hair cut or to be shaved. He used ordinary scissors and clippers and shaved people with a cut-throat razor and they paid 2d for his service. The hair that was cut off was swept straight onto the compost heap which we called the 'bumby'. Father taught my brothers the crafts he worked at and was pleased they were hard workers like him. One of my brothers made a sideboard out of old tea chests, finishing it

with paint and transfers.

Ida Cunningham

Herbert Shergold

I was born in Corporation Road in 1924. My mother died when I was seven years old. My father worked at Hoffmans as a foreman in the machine shop and my grandfather on my father's side, Herbert Shergold, worked at the *Essex Chronicle* before buying his own printing business just off Duke Street. The building is still there back behind Andrews the undertakers. You could stand in my grandad's printing place and see them making up the coffins. Later my uncle Harold took over the business. My grandparents lived in Manor Road at No. 21 and when I was four years old we moved into No. 32, so I was often at my grandparents' house.

Doris Wesley

County Surveyor

I worked at the County Surveyor's office in Arbor Lane, where the Mews flats are now. After the war I went to work at the police headquarters in Springfield Road. It was office administration work. In the 1950s I got a job in London with British Petroleum, travelling by train from Chelmsford station, often on a steam train. It was great fun as there was quite a crowd of us – we met and travelled together. I left work in 1956 when I had my son Simon.

Barbara Rayment

Crompton Parkinson

In 1939 when I was sixteen years old I passed my exams and started at Crompton Parkinson as a trainee junior draughtsman. I was one of the first people to take advantage of the day release as Crompton Parkinson joined the trainee scheme in 1939. There were two departments, electrical motors and generators. I was in the motor department and worked there until I was made redundant twenty-nine years later in 1968. During the war years we designed equipment for the war effort; although some joined the forces, we were in a reserved occupation. There was well over a hundred on the work force, including my future wife, and it was a good firm to work for with a canteen, sports and social club.

David Cook

Marconi Apprentice

I started working at Marconi's on Monday 13 April 1953 when I was fifteen years old. My wages were £1 19s 6d for a forty-three-hour week and I was an apprenticed instrument maker. Because I was under eighteen years old and not earning very much I received a reduction in train fares and could travel to and from work for about 1s 9d a day. I filled in the form and paid 29s 9d a month and would do this until I reached eighteen. When I first started travelling they were steam trains, changing over the years to diesel and finally electric. There were batches of apprentices, thirty-six at a time; some were university graduates who became the high fliers of the company. We all did a five-year apprenticeship and to be accepted on this scheme I had to go to Marconi's and sit some tests. It was my idea to apply and I went on my own.

On the factory floor there were up to 100 machines including mills, lathes and turners. Both the engraving and polishing departments had ten machines each. My first boss, the top chief inspector Mr Fish, was very nice man, not like a lot of bosses who wouldn't speak to you if they saw you outside. He treated all of us in a proper manner. Another person I remember was Mr Harry Claydon who was in charge of the progress department – he is still going strong at eighty-three years old.

Marconi's had a very well-subsidized canteen where you could buy cooked food or sandwiches; it was well used during the lunch hour. For our ten-minute tea break we rarely left our machines; most people were on piece-work so would rather not stop for the break. We either bought a flask of coffee or somebody would go over to the canteen and buy a pint mug of tea or coffee and share it with those around.

Mick Horsley

Bill Woolley, professional soldier, 1928-1950.

Full Pay of £4 17s 6d

When I came back after the war I asked at Hoffmans if my old job was still open and it was. I was then employed as a fully fledged operator on full pay of £4 17s 6d before stoppages each week. As an apprentice I worked on various machines; we would also run errands throughout the factory and we were often in trouble for riding up and down in the lifts. I went from 'J Dept' on to the production staff in the 'Y Dept', where I remained until I took voluntary redundancy in 1981. Apprentices would begin in department stores and when a vacancy came in the department if he was qualified he would go on the shop floor, although apprentices normally stayed in the store for about six months. One job was to take work to be hardened to the hardening department; another was to get tools from the tool store and also any drawings that were required for work in progress. Eventually you would be attached to an operator to learn the machines before being allowed to operate them yourself, mainly roughing machines. I found this interesting and fascinating.

Dennis Smith

Joined the Cavalry

I decided to join the Army when I was seventeen years old and me and my mate walked the twelve miles from Chelmsford to Brentwood to sign on. I was used to walking long distances and thought nothing of it. I told the recruitment officer I was eighteen and when they measured me they found I was half an inch short, but they said, 'That won't matter, you will grow.' He then asked what jobs I'd had and I told him I worked on farms. 'Can you ride a horse?' he asked, and I said 'Yeah', although the only one I'd ever sat on was an old cart horse. Anyway they put me in

Ernie Hewitt cartoons.

the cavalry. When I saw their horses stamping in the stables I thought, 'This is a bit different to what I'm used to.'

Bill Woolley

Turned Shirts

I worked at County Hall from 8.30 a.m. to 4 p.m. and earned £4 a week. They used to have a Council Day once a week. There were several lady councillors. The Medical Officer of Health brought his curtains in for me to sew; he would pay me 10s a curtain and I felt frightened to take it. Once I told him I was trying to lose weight and he said to me, 'My dear, you will never lose weight because you laugh too much.' He used to bring his shirts in for me to turn the collars when they got frayed. I did all my sewing by hand.

Molly Watson

Little Pinny

Mr Pearce was a Major and I recall he would sometimes bring back up to six soldiers for an evening meal. We ate well, although we were on rations. I did the cooking and when serving Mr Pearce and his guests would put a pinny on over my dress.

Ida Cunningham

Ernie Hewitt

When I was at Hoffman's I remember working with Ted Revell, Geoff Gulliver, Charles Brown, Kim Bone (who we called

Tombstone), Squibby Matthams, Henry Mardell, Johnny Atkinson, Nobby Rising and Eric Snowden – we were all friends. Cyril Hammond and Jim Mole were long established men who looked askance at the antics we young people got up to. I must not forget Ernie Hewitt who was foreman in the 'J Dept' and who kept everyone amused with his clever cartoon drawings.

Dennis Smith

Old Fire Station

The old fire station was on the corner of Market Road and Threadneedle Street. Before we had a television set the station had a radio that was wired to a local company, perhaps Marconi's, who had a system and we got our programmes through them. There was also a full-sized snooker table, though I didn't use it much: I was more of a darts player. We used to visit local factories and public buildings to familiarize ourselves with the layout in case they ever had a fire.

Dave Wright

CHAPTER 4

Leisure

Grace and Doug Pheasant's dancing days.

Orpheus Coffee Shop

My father worked for most of the local authorities around here. Originally he came from Wales but settled here after being demobbed from the Forces at the end of the war. He was a veteran of Arnhem and we are all very proud of him.

He bought a two-acre smallholding near Great Baddow and both he and my mum worked very hard there. We used to catch the No. 31 bus into Chelmsford – it is still the No. 31 on that route today – and go to the dances at the Corn Exchange. It always made me laugh because they used to make us put plastic caps on our stilettos so we wouldn't damage their floors. I often wondered what they did about the old farmers who went in there in their hobnailed boots. We also went for ballroom dancing lessons in a room over the Odeon, though we were forbidden from going to the Long Bar on the Baddow Road. It was used by bikers for their hang-out and there had been the odd fight or two. Another one of our favourite places was a coffee shop called Orpheus; it was in the London Road, down a flight of stairs and into a cellar. It's funny but when I was in Russia recently we went into a coffee shop just like it.

Lynne Harding

Peggy Green

We went to Hoffman's Club. Peggy Green ran that – she organized all sorts of things. It was open every night and in the summer we would go to the sports field and play tennis. They held dances at the Corn Exchange and the Shire Hall. The GIs went as well and the Corn Exchange would be jam-packed every night; there were quite a few British troops about as well as Americans. I would go every week to the cinema. We were always about doing something or other, there was always something going on.

Doris Wesley

Smuggled into the Pub

In the High Street a bit up from Freeman, Hardy & Willis there was a long passageway called Crane Court, at the end of which stood the Doris Rodd School of Dancing. Both my brother and I would go there for our regular dancing lessons. I would go to the Odeon cinema – in those days Tyrone Power and Deanne Durbin were my favourites. In the youth club we would go for a pub crawl and if anybody was underage we tried to smuggle them in. I particularly remember the Red Lion in London Road. Sometimes one of the members would take us back to her home where she got out the rhubarb wine. We were all right indoors, but floated once we were out in the fresh air! We mostly drank shandies and we never went to pubs on our own. We would all sing afterwards going down the streets. We also went on long hikes, sometimes to Baddow Meads.

Mary Woolf

Dances at Tiptree

We went to dances and social events at the fire station, where they took out the engines and had dancing in the appliance bay. When I was at the telephone exchange we would all go to dances at Tiptree. They were held upstairs in a wooden barn. For Doug, a fireman, it was awful as there was only one exit which was up narrow wooden stairs. We took our own food and we jived. It was a proper venue for dancing in the evening, but they sold strawberries there other times. There were a lot of young girls at the exchange so apart from the dancing we would also go on coach trips. Sometimes three coaches would take us up to London to the cinema to see 3D films.

Grace Pheasant

Margaret and Pete Brannan and friends.

Bob Hadler and Douglas Catt.

Stuck up a Tree

We used to go mushrooming in the fields where Rainsford school is now. We played all sorts of games and once I got stuck up a tree and my dad had to come and rescue me. In the street we would play marbles, hopscotch and hoops, we roller skated and rode our bikes. I learnt to ride my first bike around the green.

Mary Ellis

YMCA

I was more interested in boats and trains than sports though I did play tennis at the YMCA club. The courts were grass and situated down St Fabian's Drive and in a field to the left. I sometimes also played at a court in Danbury. Gilbert Torry and his sister who lived in Sandford Road were my friends. I would meet them on a Sunday to go for a

The Westlands Boys' Football Club.

hike – the pipe and walking stick type. We would go to Danbury, sometimes to the Rodney. I then learnt to fly with the Civil Air Guards at Southend Aerodrome Club. We met on a Wednesday afternoon and also on Sundays, which were my times off. It was 30s an hour, subsidized by the Civil Air Guard, and you had fifteen hours' total tuition. My first solo was after either ten or eleven hours. After the war I tried dinghy racing and later went on to bigger ships; I had a sailing yacht moored at Maldon.

Douglas Catt

The Global School of Dancing

On a Saturday we sometimes went to Fernando's hop. I also went regularly to ballroom and old-time dancing. I think it was called the Global School of Dancing and the classes were held at the Corn Exchange which has since been demolished. The teachers were a middle-aged married couple who always dressed for the part. For special presentations he always wore an evening suit and bow tie and she wore an evening dress; for competitions we wore ballroom gowns which we had either borrowed or were given as hand-me-downs, and our own silver shoes. For the lessons we wore our ordinary clothes. I did not have a regular partner, just anyone who was available, and of course there were usually more girls than boys. Over the time I was there I achieved bronze, silver and gold medals.

Nina Stanford

George and his brother at Yarmouth.

Chelmsford Boys' Club

My brother and I belonged to the Chelmsford Boys' Club. There was a hut in Rectory Lane at first, then we all helped dig the foundations for the new Boys' Club building. We played table tennis, other games and also went to camp in Yarmouth. We had to raise enough money to go to camp and for our spending money; we sold scented cards and went round the houses collecting waste paper, which was very scarce at that time. I went to Saturday morning pictures at the Odeon: it cost 5d, was very noisy and we watched mostly cowboy films.

George Christodoulou

Chelmsford Girl Guides

I was deeply involved with the Girl Guide movement from the age of twelve onwards,

the 2nd Chelmsford Company attached to London Road church. Because the captain had been ill I had been running the company. Although I was not quite nineteen when she died, under wartime allowance I was warranted as the captain, a post not usually held by some one under the age of twenty-one. The movement kept going through the war years but obviously parents of young girls were unwilling to let them out during dangerous times. There was a lot of work to do after the war as we had to try and build the numbers up again. Most of my spare time was involved with the Guide Movement.

Phyllis Everett

9-inch Television

My father-in-law bought us a television set in about 1950 and it had a 9-inch screen.

We were in a terrace of houses and everyone would crowd in to watch it. When I was a child we would play in the street chalking out hopscotch on the flagstones, and we also played with hoops and a top and whip. We made the tops pretty with bits of silver paper so that when they went round they looked lovely.

Doris Wesley

Victor Silvester

I would go to the cinema at the Select, Pavillion or Empire. I never missed *The Lone Ranger* which was on in the evenings at the Empire. I mostly watched Westerns with people like Gene Autrey in them. At the Select they had what we called 'Tuppenny Rush' in the evening. I also liked dancing; three of us – Gordon Ransom, Keith Rogers and I – learnt ballroom dancing at the

Maidie Russell School of Dancing which was down the Saracen's Head yard. We also went ballroom dancing to live bands at the Odeon which was called the Ritz in those days. I remember going to the Shire Hall when Victor Silvester came to town. Hoffmans sometimes held dances; their social club had one of the finest dance floors in East Anglia. It was where the shops are now on the university campus.

Ted Revell

Cooking Lessons

During my courting days as I couldn't cook we decided I should take lessons. Bernard met me from the cooking classes at the Technical School in Victoria Road and we would walk across the fields to Writtle.

Mary Woolf

A Chelmsford Carnival float, 1934.

Emily and William Morgan playing in the park.

Walnut Cabinet

My mother had the first television set I saw. It was a little black and white set in a beautiful walnut cabinet with doors. We all watched the Coronation, neighbours and relatives. We listened to the wireless a lot – *Twenty Questions* and *ITMA* and of course always the news. We always read the *Daily Herald*.

Mary Ellis

A Week-long Carnival

Just before the war, the Carnival would last a week. There would be a procession on Saturday and on Sunday a 'Drum Head' service on the cricket ground. The TA, British Legion, St John's, Scouts, Guides etc. would march through the town – it was quite an event. In Hall Street in my grandfather's house we had a front parlour. When I was four years old we used it when my sister got married in St John's church. I had a bunch of flowers and I thought I had married him too!

Phyllis Everett

May Day

The only holiday I remember is May Day. The kids would go to the shop and be given a bag of mixed sweets; they were normally piled in a tin bath in the doorway, one bag for each child, but some cheeky children went back for more.

Molly Watson

Baddow Meads

We cycled most places and took the local buses and trains, so I never wanted to drive. From Sunday school we had outings to Clacton and other seaside places and my parents always took us on a two-week holiday to the sea. We would go for walks and picnics in Baddow Meads which used to flood very badly. We could see the water from our home in Chelmer Road. This was rectified when they built the river defences.

Barbara Rayment

A Portable Record Player

A portable record player was really the thing to have when I was a teenager. It was called portable because it was housed in a case-like frame and had a handle for carrying. It was fairly heavy but nonetheless portable and we carried them with us when we went to see friends. Records were large and made of a brittle type of plastic; we had to be careful as they were easy to scratch or crack. We spent a lot of time swapping records, dancing and generally enjoying the music.

Mary Scott

The Tuppenny Rush

As a child we went on a Saturday afternoon to The Empire or Regent cinemas. We called it the 'Tuppenny Rush'. I saw my first 'talkie' at The Empire, Springfield Road. I remember Al Jolson, Janet Gaynor and Charles Farrell; also *Casablanca* and many other films. For 9d we had a seat and a bag of sweets. From the age of seventeen I would go to dances and parties at St John's Hospital, which used to be a workhouse before it was a hospital, and it was where my sister-in-law worked. The dances finished late and at 2 a.m. we would walk home to Springfield. We also went to the Odeon Ballroom, the Corn Exchange and to the Shire Hall for ballroom dances. Some of our courting was done in Lawn Lane – it was all fields then, right up to the farm which is now Channels Golf Club.

Ivy Holden

Galleywood Race Course

When I was at school we looked forward to the races arranged on the common. There were only about three a year but we were all given the afternoon of school so we could see the races. We used to play on the common then as there were no fears of kids being harmed. It was a full course, a two-mile track fenced off all round, with proper stands. We could see the horses as the race started and we would run across to enjoy the water jump and be back in time for the finish. The main feature was the steep uphill finish and many good horses started there, including Golden Miller, who went on to win the National.

The Parish Council agreed to another enclosure being erected in the '20s, opposite the old stand and near the winning post. This had been requested by the race managers so that they had more control over the bookies who had been setting up anywhere on the common.

As it was on common land, one of the conditions imposed was that the local people had free access to both common and the new enclosure. A local policeman who knew all the villagers was on duty and made sure there were no problems. We dashed to search the bookies' enclosure after the races, searching for any coins that had been dropped: a sixpenny find would keep us in sweets for a week.

When the steeplechase races finished in 1935 so did the half-day holidays. The 170-year history of horse racing ended, probably due to the problems of holding them on common land – as the people couldn't be charged for watching the races it became unprofitable.

David Cook

Treats for Mother

On my day off I went home and would spend some of my 6s wages on little treats for my mother. Sometimes I would take a pair of curtains, a bit of carpet or anything that Mrs Pearce offered me. In those days people in big houses that you worked for, before they threw anything away, would offer it to the staff.

Ida Cunningham

The Victoria Club

As a child my friends and I would play hide and seek and chasing games in the playing field in Woodland Road, which later became a nursery. We had dancing lessons at school in the hall which I enjoyed – we learnt country dancing. I was a member of the Baptist church; we had a youth club and different organizations which I belonged to. Later both my girls were in the Girls' Brigade – they had all sorts of activities, including a camp every year. They worked very hard to get their badges and later for the Duke of Edinburgh Award, and meetings were held at the church in Victoria Road. I helped with the Victoria Club which was set up to help people in need. They came to us through Social Services and I helped with the lunches. On Friday mornings they also had a crèche for children up to the age of five; mums were invited to come in for coffee and I helped with the coffees. After my experience at the florist I have always been a keen gardener. At home with my father I pottered around and looked after the garden although my brother-in-law came to do the vegetables.

Gladys Hilliard

Ockelford Avenue

Outside the school gates and in Ockelford Avenue and North Avenue we would play marbles and five stones in the street; we also exchanged cigarette cards. I played with Les Gilroy, Dennis Wood, Alan Butcher and Geoff Hurst, the World Cup-winning footballer – he lived on the Chignal Estate. Later I did a paper round on the Chignall Estate for 'Wells'; it was always muddy up there so they supplied me with big wellingtons and a yellow cape.

George Christodoulou

The £1 Share

We went to the Wheatsheaf in New Street but mostly used the bar in the Hoffmans

Ted and his wife Ada May at the final.

factory club. My husband went every Saturday to watch Chelmsford City play football. Years ago my father bought a £1 share in the football ground.

Doris Wesley

Phone Lessons

My friend Hilda Ashdown and I joined the Girls' Training Corps, which held their meetings at the High School. We wore a navy blouson, navy skirt and a little hat. We went out in groups to learn how to use the phone in the public phone box in Corporation Road. We also learnt Morse code.

Mary Ellis

Boys' Brigade

When I moved to Chelmsford I was in the Chelmsford 3rd Company Boys' Brigade at Victoria Road Baptist church. In the Chelmsford area there were five companies of the Boys' Brigade. I wore a white lanyard over ordinary clothes, and shorts and later grey trousers. In the early days we wore a pillar box hat. When I worked at the Model Laundry I took the van to the carnival twice; I drove it all decorated up. the carnival started in Rectory Lane then went along Broomfield Road into the town to Moulsham Street and London Road where the Carnival Queen would go into the hospital. We finished up in Central Park for the fair, fireworks and dancing.

Ted Revell

George and his brother in Ockelford Avenue.

Blue Spot Assembly Kit

Chelmsford at that time was a country town and I remember going in the fields with a friend whose father worked at Marconi's and playing around with a crystal set. The first time I saw a set with valves was when we assembled one from a 'Blue Spot do-it-yourself assembly kit'. At first we could only get a faint sound, but then someone had the bright idea of attaching a long piece of wire from the set to the barbed wire fence and the reception was brilliant. We told everyone who then came to the field to hear it for themselves. I remember the big radio mast being put up at Baddow, which was the highest point round here. We went up to get any odd jobs that were going so we could earn a few coppers.

Bill Woolley

Hoffmans Sports and Social Club

Hoffmans had a thriving sports and social club in Bishops Hall Lane, now a shopping precinct on the university campus. The workforce were expected to belong: apprentices were stopped 1d a week and operatives 3d a week [to pay for the club]. You could take part in any of the activities run by the social club, including ballroom dancing, opera, drama, wine, horticulture, cycling, athletics and debating, among many other pastimes. There were rooms in the building I never knew existed, as well as a stage and dressing room for the drama group. The apprentices used to put a float in the Carnival and one big event of the year was the inter-factory athletics meeting which took place in Colchester, Brentwood and Chelmsford – all the factories in the area participated. One event was held in St Fabian's sports ground. Hoffmans also had their own sports day and hockey, cricket and football tournaments.

Dennis Smith

Local Pubs

After we played cricket we would drink in the Bull opposite Admirals Park and after watching football we went into the Bird in the Hand in New Writtle Street. Sometimes we'd go to the Two Brewers and of course the factories had their own social clubs with bars. My father went to the Three Elms in Chignal on Friday and Saturday. When he was working, during the week, I'd go down to get him a pint of Old Mild at 4½d a pint and ten Players for my brother at 6d a packet. When I was fourteen I had my first packet of cigarettes.

Ted Revell

Saturday Night

After work on a Saturday night we often went to Boreham village hall for dancing. It cost 1s to get in and there was always a singer as well as live music. We were always happy to change from our uniforms into the tiered skirts with flounced lacy petticoats, stiletto shoes and herringbone tights that were all the rage then.

Maureen Wiseman

Dennis Smith in 1939.

Betty Grable

There were no leisure activities at all except the cinema as a treat once a fortnight. We went to the Odeon where the best seats cost 1s 9d. I remember Betty Grable was all the rage then and a film called *The Man in Grey*.

Molly Watson

Round the Horne

When I was a schoolgirl I went to the cinema on a Saturday afternoon to see Tom Mix in a cowboy film. Later I went twice a week to either the Empire, the Odeon, the Regent, the Pavillion or the Select. Sometimes we would all sit round the wireless and listen to *Round the Horne*. At school on May Day we had a maypole which we all danced around.

Sally Pattendon

Dancing by the River

Courting couples went to Lawn Lane which is now a housing estate but then was a country lane. When I was small I went to Sunday school at Trinity church and later belonged to the youth club which met in

George Christodoulou (centre) at the seaside.

the church hall; we played table tennis and went on hikes. I played tennis on the courts in Springfield and swam in both the outdoor pool and in the river – like lots of children we swam in any accessible place. Carnival day was a big occasion in those days, we would watch the procession from Victoria Road before going on to the fair and later joining in the dancing on the river bank. The whole day was wound up with a big firework display.

Barbara Rayment

Chelmsford Town Carnival

I enjoyed both cricket and football but with my job and part-time education I had little time to spare. During the war years I was conscripted into the Home Guard. We met in various places including the Methodist church in Baddow Road and the London Road Congregational church. My courting days followed this: we cycled into Chelmsford to the cinemas – the Regent, Odeon, Select and Pavilion. I remember watching *Gone With The Wind*, *Burma Victory* and all the Road films.

When my parents were young in the 1920s the Regent put on music-hall entertainment. We also used to watch the Chelmsford Town Carnival; between the wars it was run specifically for the benefit of the hospitals. A lot of effort went into them and the procession would halt outside the London Road Hospital, and of course, as now, there was a fun fair afterwards.

David Cook

Choirboy

I had a crystal radio set at home and I listened to music. I was also a choirboy in the Cathedral. When I was eleven, we got paid something like 12s a quarter; we were paid an extra 2s 6d for weddings and 3s for funerals, and for Sunday morning services that were broadcast on the BBC we got 3s. Clive Plumb who was the top soprano in our choir was chosen to sing at the Coronation.

George Christodoulou

YMCA

When I was fifteen and sixteen years old I went to the Chelmsford YMCA, in the same building as they use today. From Monday to Saturday we could play billiards, snooker or table tennis. They had their own sports field up St Fabian's Drive and I played cricket for them. Reg Sleat, Gordon Ranson, Ray Ranson and Keith Rogers were also in the team. Later I played for both Hoffmans and Marconis.

Ted Revell

Back Row Courting

On a Saturday night we would go to Fernando's in the town where they had a band. The seats were placed all round the central dance floor. We all hung our coats in the cloakroom and I don't remember anything ever being stolen. I remember one shift dress that I bought at a shop in Silver End – it cost £2 which I borrowed off my dad. I paid him back at 10s a week.

Three of the cinemas we went to were the Regent (which is now 'Chicago's'), the Select and the Odeon. *South Pacific*, *The Sound of Music*, *Parent Trap* and *Whistle down the Wind* were some of my favourite musicals.

The usherettes always stood at the front in the intermission, shining a torch onto their tray from which you could buy choc ices, ice cream tubs and orange drinks in round cardboard cups. Young people used to clamour to get in the back row at cinemas where a lot of courting was done.

Above the Odeon was a very big room where dances were held every Sunday evening. David Thoroughgood and Paul Brown (Nobby) were two boys from Witham that were in the band. The room had a big silver ball hanging in the middle; it reflected all the light and of course it was very crowded.

Margaret Brannan

Margaret Brannan in the 1960s.

Corpus Christi

Corpus Christi, which we called the May Day procession, was where a statue of the Virgin Mary was carried up Moulsham Street and down London Road to the Catholic church. The statue was then carried inside to be crowned. All the children went into the church to watch the crowning. They all carried baskets of flowers – they were narcissi and, oh, the smell was wonderful! They then sang 'Oh Mary we crown thee with blossoms today, Queen of the angels and Queen of the may'.

Molly Watson

All the Works Went to Walton

When the children were young we would go on holiday to a guest house in Walton; we went on the bus from Chelmsford. The buses would be chock-a-block – all the works went to Walton so you always met people you knew. We sometimes went on coach outings and to Clacton once or twice.

Mollie Smith

Muffin the Mule

I was in the Girl Guides and became a Girl Guide captain. I also joined the Band of Hope when I was quite young sometimes the meetings were held at the school. My parents bought the first television set I ever saw – it was a little black and white one. Both my child and my brother's child would watch *Muffin the Mule*: they went very close to the eight or nine-inch screen and they both cried when the programme finished and the television was switched off.

Ivy Holden

Chelmsford Cricket Ground

I was very keen on cricket and have always supported the Essex team who play at the Chelmsford ground. When I first bought a season ticket it cost £48; now the cost is £77. I never had a lot of spending money but Marconi's was right opposite the cricket ground and I got full value for my season ticket by going over to the ground during my lunch hours. In 1960 I took a week's holiday to watch the team play at the Clacton ground.

Mick Horsley

Lionmead Courts

I played both hockey and tennis at school, and for pleasure I played tennis at the Lionmead Courts. I went 'tiddler fishing' down the river by Victoria Road. We always went to see the carnival and I entered it once or twice when I was a member of the Guides. After the carnival there was the fun fair, followed by dancing on the recreation ground at night. We had social evenings in the Social Hall at Hoffmans. During the war a lot of American soldiers from Wethersfield would go to the dances. I was married then but several girls from Hoffmans went out with them and a lot married and became GI brides.

Ivy Holden

Ub Smith and Percy Barnard with the Army Cadets.

1935 Silver Jubilee

The 1935 Silver Jubilee Day festivities took place on the football ground. Schools took part and my brother was in the physical education display. I played a drum. We marched in lines onto the football field and played our musical instruments, there was community singing encouraged by the teacher, and we sang 'A Health unto His Majesty' with gusto. We could not see anything as we were behind the football stadium.

Phyllis Everett

Social Club Discount Card

I went with my husband to dances and social evenings at the Hoffman's social club.

At Christmas there had to be two nights devoted to the socials as so many people wanted to go they couldn't all fit in on one evening. It was free, with a beautiful buffet. There was also a children's Christmas party and they put on trips to London to take the children to pantomimes. I remember going to see *Mr Pastry on Ice*. We had a discount card from the social club, and stores participated including Webbers & Bollingbroke. Some stores gave 10 per cent and some 20 per cent discount.

Mollie Smith

CAODS

My parents started the Chelmsford Amateur Operatic and Drama Society of which I am still

Freddie Munion and CAODS.

a Vice-President. They started before the war and the society is still going strong. I have sung in the chorus and my mother used to sing in their productions at the Empire Theatre which was next to the iron bridge at Springfield Road. This theatre no longer exists. Sometimes she also performed at the Regent which later became a cinema and is now a 'rock-type café'. We always had a piano and I was taught at an early age and still play occasionally. A chap called Freddie Munion used to be in a lot of productions, often taking the lead in comedies.

Douglas Catt

Ovaltinies

We had a television set when they first came out – it was black and white in a tall wooden cabinet. I remember watching the Coronation and others came in and watched it with us. We listened to the radio a lot and my sister and I were Ovaltinies. We also played with hoops and spinning tops and generally made our own fun. As a child I went to both the Ritz and Regent cinemas; we usually went to matinée performances. At Christmas we always had a children's Christmas party. My mother and father would put up the decorations on Christmas Eve and we had a stocking at the end of the bed which was always filled with little bits and pieces. My mother made her own Christmas cake and mince pies and she always put a silver threepenny bit in the pudding. Various relations would come round and eat with us over the holiday.

Barbara Rayment

Congregational Chapel

As a child I went to the Congregational Chapel opposite Springfield School. It was part of the big one in London Road, which is now Christ Church. We went on a Sunday afternoon and I remember Miss Bell and her brother who taught us. We sang a hymn accompanied on the piano, then had a scripture lesson, after which they gave us texts. I think we went on trips to Maldon by horse and cart.

Sally Pattendon

Coronations

On Coronation Day, May 12th 1937, it poured with rain. There were amusements and a fun fair at the top of Central Park. All schoolchildren had a book of tickets for free rides and we were also given free drinks and a bag of cakes which we had to collect. My friend and I travelled up to the Festival of Britain in London in 1951. When it was the Queen's Coronation in 1953 we had a day off from work and we watched it on television at our neighbours'; they lived below us in Tudor Road and we didn't have a television set then.

Phyllis Everett

Rainsford Youth Centre

At fourteen I joined the youth centre at Rainsford. We did concert parties for old people's homes and hospitals and we sang, played charades and did little sketches. There were about twenty to twenty-four young people. I was a member for about five years, eventually becoming Chairman of the committee in 1950. Geoff Hurst was Vice Chairman; he was a lovely fellow, quietly spoken. He later married a Chelmsford girl and, as everyone knows, he went on to score in the famous 1966 World Cup Final.

George Christodoulou

All Saints' Church

I was brought up to go to Sunday school every week, we went to All Saints' church and were given prizes for learning texts from the Bible, among other things. I started as a Sunday school teacher when I was eighteen

Douglas Catt in fancy dress.

years old. I also belonged to the church youth club which held social evenings and dances.

Ivy Holden

Chelmsford City

I started watching Chelmsford City play football before the war, and in 1968 I formed the Chelmsford Mini League. I later ran the Chelmsford youth team. I have had a long association with Chelmsford City and the touth team. I trained Nigel Spinks who played for Westlands Boys then Chelmsford before moving on to Aston Villa. There was Mark Delalavic who went on to play for Wimbledon, and Gary Goodchild who later

played for Arsenal and Hereford. Chelmsford City players included Paul Marlow, Kim Yates, Kevin Foster and Phil Thrift. After the war I ran the Co-op cricket club and played for Hoffmans second team. I played cricket until I was sixty.

Ted Revell

The 'Animals'

I remember spending a lot of time in the Orpheus coffee bar when it was the 'in' place for young people to gather. Also later in the Lion and Lamb in Duke Street, which we called the 'Animals' – this was a venue for teenagers in the '60s. In the High Street opposite Springfield Road was an old pub

Chelmsford City youth team.

OFFICIAL HANDBOOK
OF THE
CHELMSFORD CITY
FOOTBALL CLUB
●
SEASON 1938-9   PRICE 3d.

Front cover of the Chelmsford City
Football Club handbook.

and we would meet in the room above for
the Folk Club. They had live acts there, like
Bert Jantz, Nadia Cattouse, many top
names, and a great atmosphere where you
could chat to the performers. Many of them
that did the folk club circuit went on to be
big names. Upstairs in the Odeon Ballroom
they had regular traditional jazz gigs, it was
always packed out as they featured mostly
well known bands. Chelmsford had its
cinemas and live music venues but very
little in the way of places to eat out. That is
all remedied now, there are plenty of wine
bars, cafés, restaurants and coffee houses.

Diane Watson

CHAPTER 5

Shops

George at Hillside Stores.

W.F. Catt & Son

My mother was an Underwood; her father –
my grandfather – bought a plot of land on
the corner of Wells Street and Dukes Street
where he built a butcher's shop with
accommodation above. My other
grandfather had a family grocers in Tindal

Square that was called W.F. Catt & Son and
my father also had a family grocery store in
Moulsham Street which was called W.R.
Catt & Son.

Private family grocers were beginning to
go: there was no living in it and retailing
was changing with all the large stores
opening up. In 1945 as a result of town

planning the shop in Moulsham Street was compulsorily purchased, although it was another two years before development began on the new inner ring road or parkway.

Douglas Catt

Dipped Measuring Jugs

The milkman drove a horse-drawn float with churns and a bar with measuring jugs. He shouted 'Milko'. We took our jug out to the float where he dipped out the milk, we then put the milk in a cold place, perhaps a cold slab in the pantry. If it was hot weather we 'scalded' the milk at night and just hoped it wouldn't be sour in the morning. When we were in Moulsham Street a little short man would come round with a basket on his arm selling fruit; the baker also came with a basket which had a large array of bread in it. Also in Moulsham Street there was a pork butcher called Green, a beef butcher and a fishmonger called South. We had a range that burnt coal and the coal was delivered by horse and cart. The coal man used a sack on the back of his head and shoulders as protection before hoisting the laden sack onto his shoulders, he then had to take it down to the cellar in the dark.

Phyllis Everett

International Store

My mother bought most of her groceries from the International on the High Street. She thought the assistants who worked there were very polite. I can still remember the wonderful smell – I suppose it was a mixture of the cheeses, hams and other cold meats that lined the counters and added to the aroma of the various coffee beans that were on sale. The assistants did all the walking around then: the customer just asked for what they wanted and the girls fetched it, always showing you and asking for your approval before it was wrapped. I seem to remember there was always a chair available for older customers to sit on while they waited to be served. I worked at Boots on a part-time basis for a little while; I liked it despite having to go up and down some rickety old stairs to the store room. We had small wooden two-drawer tills with a sales and receipt pad on the top – we had to write our transactions down and at the end of the day the money in our till had to agree with what we'd written down. There were other young people working there and we seemed to have a lot of fun.

Mary Scott

Hugh Wright

In Springfield Road, almost opposite to where Tesco's now stands, there was a slaughterhouse and a row of little shops. Mr and Mrs Bateman ran a dairy there; Mr Bateman was the milkman and he had a motorbike and sidecar, but where the sidecar should have been was a flat surface which held the churn of milk. He came round the houses and poured the milk we bought into our jugs. Mrs Bateman later opened a general store further on down the road. We had a greengrocer who came round on Saturday mornings with his horse and cart. I think he came from Brook End and grew a lot of his own produce. Hugh Wright was our butcher – he had several shops and delivered the meat with a horse and two-wheeled trap. Mr Wright later became Mayor of Chelmsford and every Christmas came to our school and gave all the children chocolate.

Sally Pattendon

Scotsman's Shop

Mr Pennack's daughter would pay me 2d for running errands. I would spend it in the Scotsman's shop, where it bought me six cakes which I took home and shared with the family.

Bobby Jackson, I seem to remember, was a very little man who had a cobbler's shop in Baddow High Street; it backed onto the church. My dad mended all our shoes so we never needed to use him. Silas Jackson (no relation to Bobby) was the local taxi driver; he had an old fashioned car with a soft hood. He also kept bees and sold honey. Opposite the Blue Lion was Atterbury's, a little corner shop which sold sweets and tobacco. Their daughter Doris, who was an only child, was my best friend.

Ida Cunningham

Crompton Parkinson

At fifteen I left school and went to Crompton Parkinson as a trainee in the switchgear department. My first wage was £1 6s 9d a week. I stayed one year and then went to work as a trainee butcher with the Co-op in Kings Road. As a trainee butcher I earned £4 19s 6d and one year later I went to work for Dewhurst in Brentwood. I cycled to Brentwood on my bike – it was one of those upright ones. The following year a manager at Dewhurst bought the old Co-op butcher's in Kings Road and it was renamed Jack Stevens'. I went back and worked there until I was thirty years old. In 1967 while still working at the butcher's I bought a sweet shop in Baddow Road called the Chocolate Box. In 1969 I bought a general store at Hillside Grove. I got married that year and we lived above the shop. Later I won an award for selling the most ice cream in the Essex area.

George Christodoulou

Lisle Stockings

There were no supermarkets and it was a pleasure to go shopping in them days and be served over the counter. Anything that was on ration you didn't have to worry about if you were working because the shopkeeper saved it for you until the evening. If it was bananas or oranges they would save one for each child. There were no nylon stockings; we bought what we called lisle stockings at 1s a pair. Cheese came in big vat things and it was cut by wire attached to a piece of wood; they would cut it right to the ounce. Rice was sold on the big weighing scales – they served rice like they served sweets, always separately in pounds or quarter-pounds, whatever you wanted.

Molly Watson

Brown's of Great Waltham

Our groceries were delivered by Brown's of Great Waltham. Their van driver Mr Smith would come round with a list of available produce collecting people's orders. My mother chose the goods she wanted and Mr

CHELMSFORD. — OLD HOUSES, FRIARS PLACE.

Old houses, Friars Place.

Smith would make the delivery the next day, it was a really good personal service.

Ted Revell

Pedigree Pram

Denny's in Moulsham Street and another old shop on the corner of New Writtle Street sold all sorts of things, like Smith's. Bond's was a bit higher class. At Luckin Smith's, a hardware shop, we thought it wonderful to be able to buy a glass dish, and when news got round everyone would dash down there. We bought sheets and blankets with a utility mark. I believe when you got married you received extra coupons to buy essentials. When my daughter was born in 1947 they had brought in plastic baths, shaped like half an egg, for babies. My father went to Ryder's – a quite expensive shop –

to buy a plastic bath and while he was there he was offered a big pedigree pram, which he bought. They were hard to get hold of and I was lucky and the envy of the others.

Doris Wesley

Self & Hicks

I was born in Galleywood in 1923 and moved to Writtle when I was about two or three years old. My father had a shop in Chelmsford High Street, called Saltmarsh & Son, next to Freeman, Hardy & Willis that later became Ripon's. The other side were a couple of dear old ladies, Miss Self and Miss Hicks, and their shop was called Self & Hicks and they sold baby clothes. Saltmarsh & Son were seedsmen and florists; they also did wreaths and bouquets and decorated hotels and function rooms.

They sold seeds and each kind of seed was weighed in an envelope so you could buy half an ounce of seed. As a teenager I helped out my mother who also worked in the shop.

Mary Woolf

Waggled his Wings

I had pocket money of 6d a week which I spent on sweets in Sturgeon's on the corner; it was later called Rockers. Audrey Sturgeon was courting at the beginning of the war and her boyfriend was an airman called Laurie Rocker. We thought it was wonderful when he flew his plane down low over North Avenue and waggled the wings, but he got into terrible trouble for that.

Mary Ellis

New Dining Room Suite

Chelmsford Co-op had many departments including a big furniture department. When Pete and I first got married we went to the Co-op to choose our dining room suite. It was too much to pay for in one go and it took us a year to pay it off on weekly terms. Most young marrieds had to buy big items on hire purchase in this way. It was the only new thing we bought for our home and we were very proud of it.

Margaret Brannan

Rankin's

We would walk to the town and we did our shopping at the Co-op because mother was a member. We never bought clothes from there though, as mother made them and they were all passed down. We went to Rankin's, near the Regent cinema – they sold haberdashery, cottons, lace and all sorts of thread. Next door was Hawkes' Confectionery who sold sweets which they made in their sweet factory near the railway station. My mother applied for a job for me at the factory but there were no vacancies at the time.

Ida Cunningham

Marzipan Tea Cakes

My mum would sometimes give my older sister and me a halfpenny. I would go to Everett's and buy sherbert dabs or liquorice sticks and sometimes marzipan tea cakes which were lovely. The sweets were in large jars and the shopkeeper would weigh them up. At the front of the counter was a glass case with chocolate bars in it – these were out of our reach and also too dear for us to buy.

Sally Pattendon

A Cottage Restaurant

I remember on Tindal Street there was a cottage restaurant and Wainwright's on the corner where you could buy milk drinks and ice creams. Cramphorn's had a tiny old place there too, Spalding's was opposite the Shire Hall – they sold toys and baby equipment. Another baby shop was Ryder's, up Moulsham Street, where you could take dolls to be repaired. In the High Street there was a restaurant called Williams where you got a lovely cup of tea and they also had a coal fire. I did my shopping at the Co-op including clothes, then there was Bond's as well. As a child our milk was delivered by horse and cart and the milk man filled our jugs at the door. The baker came with lovely hot rolls – I think it may have been Follet's from Broomfield.

Gladys Hilliard

Making Clothes

When we lived on Westlands there was a Co-op at the corner of Writtle Road and Waterhouse Lane where I did some of my shopping. In the town was Sainsbury's, International, Perks, Lipton's and Maypole all in the High Street. The goods were mostly weighed up and Sainsbury's had a track system which ran above your head and went to the cashier. People got to know the assistants that served them but when self service started all these smaller shops closed down. I made all my children's clothes as well as my own. Smith's, which was next to Sacks & Brendlaw, sold material; so did Bond's and the Co-op. They also sold the cotton and threads that were needed. I had a Singer machine, a hand one which had been converted to a treadle, which had been given to me by an aunt. I later had an electric one.

Mollie Smith

Rag and Bone Man

I remember the milkman who delivered was Mr Chaplin who lived at Galleywood. He had a horse and cart with a big churn from

Douglas Catt, today.

which we filled our jugs. He always wore a bowler hat. The baker also delivered and the rag and bone man came round every week. He would shout 'any old rags!' and if you had eaten rabbit he would buy the skin.

Doris Wesley

Mr Wray the Shop Walker

I would buy clothes in Bond's (now Debenhams). Bond's was a high class shop and in those days they had a shop walker. His name was Mr Wray and he dressed formally, wearing pin-striped trousers with a long tailed jacket and even white gloves. Mr Wray would open the door for the customer, bow slightly and say, 'Can I assist you in any way, ma'am?'. It was his job to provide a personal touch, especially to regular and valued customers.

Mary Woolf

Cashier's Pulley

At the Co-op your money would be put in a round 'dolly'. When the assistant pulled the pulley it shot across the room to the cashier who took your money out, put the change in then pulled another lever which shot it back across the shop to the assistant; it was wonderful. It was really interesting to go shopping then because you had personal contact with people, unlike in the supermarkets of today. Although they were hard times and money was short, I enjoyed shopping.

Molly Watson

W. Ralph Catt, grocer.

Pennyworth of Toffees

When I was a child there was a sweet shop near by. I had no pocket money but my father would take me in for a pennyworth of Golden Ray toffees in a paper twist, or a Sherbet Dab. There were big jars full of sweets – I would look at them all and keep everyone in the shop waiting.

When I was quite young in Moulsham Street, I loved to go to the market to see the animals. My mother would push me in my push chair. I never called it Market Day but I referred to it as 'Piggy Day'; mum would take me all amongst the animals in Market Road. The rabbits and chickens would be on one side, with larger animals on the other, and there were stalls at the back of the Golden Fleece, where the public toilets are today. I particularly remember the sweet stall, this had an acetylene lamp which was always lit up. The stall holder was a tall man who wore a boater and a sparkling white apron. We never went past his stall – we always stopped.

Phyllis Everett

Travelling Salesmen

In those days, pre-war, we bought our stock mainly from travelling salesmen. Sugar was always sold loose; we then weighed it and put it into 1lb or 2lb bags. During my time at Southend they began to deliver it ready packed, but this was not welcomed by the staff as it meant they might be out of their jobs. We bought chests of tea which again we packed ourselves, and loose pepper which we also weighed and packed ourselves. 2lb of sugar for example was 1s 2d, the best cheddar was 3s 6d and the other cheese 11d a pound.

There were two methods for us to make our free deliveries to customers: either by van or cycle. Before I left school Charles Rolfe was the driver of the delivery van. He lived in a cottage in Railway Street and had worked for my grandfather – you could call him an old retainer. Cycle deliveries were made by an errand boy who often cycled out to get the order, packed it and cycled back to deliver it. We often had to wait for our money, sometimes as long as a month. I lived in and received 10s 6d a week pocket money.

Douglas Catt

Payne's Photographers

During the war we often went to a little café over Spalding's toy shop in the High Street near the Saracens Head; Spalding's also did photography. When I got married we had to go to the photographers as in those days they didn't come to you. We went to Payne's opposite the bus station but he had a sort of chalet at the back of the church which he used as a studio. It was the 'in' thing to go to Payne's to have your photo taken. There was a little photographer called Stiff's in Tindal Street where I took the children for their photographs.

Doris Wesley

Miss McNair

During the war we arranged our hair as best we could – the weather did the rest. Miss McNair had a salon in the old Tindal part of Chelmsford where I later had my hair shampooed and set. I took my children to the Market Road cattle

Drinking men.

Shire Hall.

market; it was quite exciting because the cows and pigs would sometimes escape. I didn't go much to the other stalls. I went to Sainsbury's and Smith's in the High Street and I liked a little shop called Duncan's which was in the triangle between the High Street and London Road. I also loved going to Caton's sweet shop and the Wainwright Milk Bar where we could buy a strawberry milkshake, which was a new thing then.

Mary Woolf

Stockwells Hairdresser

The cattle market was opposite the fire station in Market Road. Friday was market day and I liked to go round the stalls and also took the children to see the animals. My niece worked in Stockwells in London Road – it was a hairdresser. I went there to have my hair cut; I probably had my first perm when I was about fourteen.

Gladys Hilliard

Ration Book to Sturgeon's

I would take the ration book to Sturgeon's in Kings Road to buy sweets. Also in Kings Road there was a greengrocer called Hymas & Wells, an ironmongery called Rocker's and a paper shop called Ripon's. When I was twelve I did a paper round; it covered Kings Road, Corporation Road and half of Brownings Avenue. I got paid 5s a week but a Sunday round was worth 6s. I started around six in the morning and it took roughly two hours.

George Christodoulou

Grace Pheasant in the WAAF.

Fire Stations in the War

During the war there were eight stations in Chelmsford. The fire service took over garages – Easton's garage was one, they had big heavy unit pumps there. Station 1 was Market Road and Easton's garage. Station 2 was Staple Grove, a big house in new Writtle Street. Station 3 was Hoare's garage in Rainsford Road where Chrysler's is now.

Station 4 was in Springfield Road over the bridge where Tesco's is now. All these stations had sub-stations. During the war we would always be on call. A column would be called for and there were ten pumps to a column under one officer and subs. Sometimes we would be called out as far as Barkingside but would not necessarily be needed.

Pete Huckle

Grace and Doug Pheasant (right) in 1999.

My First Banana

I was four when the war finished and my two most outstanding memories are of the terrifying tension that was in the air when the doodlebugs went silent, while we waited to see where it would land, and my first banana. My mother had promised us something wonderful and we could hardly wait to peel it, but none of us liked it so it was a disappointment all round.

Mary Scott

Aircraft Apprentice

In 1937 I joined the Air Force at the minimum age of fifteen and a quarter years as an aircraft apprentice at RAF Holton in

Bucks. I stayed in for sixteen years; I was in the Gold Coast (Ghana) for two years, and two and a half years in India. As I had signed an engagement of twelve years, at the end of the British Raj I was seconded to the Pakistan Air Force for ten months, eventually flying back to Egypt and sailing from Suez to Southampton. On return we should have had the choice from three postings near home but nobody ever got them and I was sent to Wales.

Doug Pheasant

Burning Incendiary Bombs

I was born in 1933 and grew up in Railway Street where the car park is now. My grandparents lived next door and we lived in Nos 6 and 7. I was the eldest of three boys and was seven years old when the war started. My father, who was a motor mechanic, went to serve in the Army as a despatch rider. Hoffmans and Marconi were both targets so there were a lot of bombing raids on Chelmsford. I remember me and my mates picking up shrapnel. We used to collect it in the empty baby milk tins – the council gave free powdered milk to babies in wartime – and we then swapped the bits with other boys. On the way to school we often saw burning incendiary bombs lying against the walls of the factory. They contained magnesium so it was not possible to put them out with water, so the authorities, probably the National Fire Service, covered them with sand and let them burn themselves out.

Bert Youell

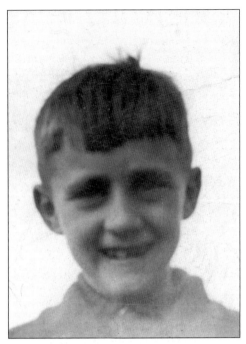

Bert Youell as a child.

Patrol Stations

At the beginning of the war, before I was called up, I was one of the men who spent two or three nights at the Surrey Docks. We went to offer some relief to the London brigade. I was off duty when Hoffmans was bombed. During the war we had patrol stations scattered round Chelmsford; this way each shift was spread out as far as possible. One was at Halls Garage in Rainsford Road. After the war there was still a patrol station at Springfield where the Little Chef is now.

Harold Wakelin

King and Queen

On VE Day we went up to London on the train and made our way to Buckingham Palace. We waited for the King and Queen to come out on the balcony to wave to the crowds. It was packed and so hot and we had to wait for ages, but it was so exciting being in that crowd that I wouldn't have missed it for anything. All the way back on the train we could look out and see how everyone was celebrating the end of the war with street parties and bonfires.

Doris Wesley

Tommy Handley

We used to listen to the radio – the news and Tommy Handley. The system was that we were wired to a local firm then for a rental fee we received programmes from them. As boys we used to collect ball bearings as we used them for making trolleys and other things. We went over the fence at Hoffmans collecting as many as we could before leaving. There was a disused air-raid shelter on some waste ground where we stacked our loot. One day there were two extra boxes and when we looked inside we could see they were full of hand grenades. A policeman arrived before any harm was done; I think some bloke found them and lugged them into the shelter for safety.

Bert Youell

Norwich

At eighteen years old I became a fireman; it was in 1942 during the war. I remember Hoffmans being hit when sixteen were killed. Also when we were going to Norwich, a whole column of us, the town seemed alight from end to end. The main hospital had evacuated all the beds and equipment on to the grass outside; we were there five nights. They had rendezvous points including a golf course that was taken over and we got our meals there. The Canadian Red Cross supplied mobile canteens. We usually slept where we could but the arrangements were very good. A lot of breweries were taken over so you got as much beer as you liked and it was warm. There was a great deal of comradeship during the war.

Pete Huckle

Bombs at Hoffmans

I volunteered with my school friend Bob Hadler. I spent two years in England then in 1942 I was sent via South Africa to Egypt.

From Cairo I was posted to Sicily and followed the Eighth Army back to Europe. A chipped tooth was my only war wound. At one point I was posted to Great Leighs and could catch the bus into Chelmsford to see my family. I was demobbed while I was in Norway before returning home to Chelmsford. People at home had a bad time of it and some bombs had fallen round Hoffmans.

Douglas Catt

A Night Bomber

Just before the war we moved to a flat in a block in Coval Lane. One night in May 1941, at 1.15 a.m., with no warning at all, a lone enemy bomber dropped a large bomb. We think it was aimed at the viaduct but it landed on sheds to the rear. The neighbouring block of flats collapsed like a pack of cards and came to rest against the wall of our block. Mum yelled at me to get under the bed and piece of ceiling hit me on the head. Several people were killed in the other block so we were lucky. We had no roof or windows and I will never forget the sound of that collapse. It was like a hose pipe playing stones, not water, on the windows. We went to live with my brother further down the road until our old landlord offered us a flat in Tudor Avenue.

Phyllis Everett

Hoffmans Memorial

Before I was married we moved in 1939 from Manor Road to Loftin Way. The first bomb I remember being dropped was when I was walking the dogs round Loftin Way – of course it was all fields then. I heard a terrific explosion when a bomb fell on a house in Beehive Lane. I was so scared I ran all the way home, but later we all got used to it. Hoffmans was bombed often, mainly at night or on weekends when the office staff weren't there, but one night a bomb dropped on the Cage Department and many were killed. There is a memorial near the crematorium in their honour. I think that happened on December 14th. There were so many workers employed making munitions and bits of planes it was very busy and lots of mothers worked at night when their children were in bed.

Doris Wesley

Machine-gunned in the Street

I went to Victoria Road School and when the siren sounded during lessons the teachers would march us to the air-raid shelter in the graveyard of the Cathedral. It was made of concrete and built against the wall of the Cathedral school. During one of these raids a mother came and took her child out of the shelter as she wanted to go home. The teachers told us later that a German plane had flown in low and machine gunned them as they walked up the street; they were both dead.

Bert Youell

War Service

When I was eighteen and a half I was called up into the Army. Harold Wakelin had already gone into the RAF. We were reserved in the Fire Service up to twenty-four years old

Army Lance Corporal Revell is standing on the left, with Keith Fletcher and Maurice Cornish next to him. Higgins is in the driver's seat.

though we were all under that age when we went. I was posted to North Africa with the Royal Berkshire Regiment. I went to Sicily and Italy, and I was wounded in Anzio. The regiment was broken up and I went into the Royal Fusiliers and then the Royal Ordnance Corps before coming home to England under the PYTHON system (prolonged service overseas). Before I was demobbed I spent eight weeks in Bicester where I met my wife to be, Thelma. She was in the ATS. When I was back in Chelmsford and travelled up to Bicester to visit Thelma frequently. We got married on New Year's Eve 1947 in Chelmsford Registry Office – we've been married now for fifty-three years.

Pete Huckle

Coval Lane First Aid Post

When I left school the war started. We had left Writtle just before the war but my father still kept his nurseries there. We moved to the other side of Chelmsford but my father said that we all ought to keep together, so we all went to live above the shop in the High Street. Soon afterwards, the lease ran out and we all moved to Duke Street opposite the Cathedral and lived in the rooms above the shop for the duration of the war. I joined the Women's Land Army during 1940, and as I was already doing market gardening they sent me to Waltham Abbey. When my father became ill I asked for compassionate posting and was sent to Writtle College which was then called the War Agricultural Committee. All the landscaping was dug up to grow potatoes and cabbages etc. Yet again I was cycling to work but going the other way this time. I stayed there until 1945. We had to be very adaptable during the war years. One night Chelmsford had been blitzed when we were in Duke Street. I had done a bit of first aid in Coval Lane and as I was in the shop I went to the front door and could see things were on fire. I put on a tin hat and dungarees and headed for the first aid post in Coval Lane. As I crossed Duke Street to the corner of Victoria Road I could see that the Cannons restaurant was on fire. There were fire engines there and as I crossed to the railway station side I could see the RAF with a barrage balloon. An RAF man swore at me, I looked at him and said 'Coval Lane first aid post,' and he said, 'I'm so sorry ma'am, I thought you were a man'. So nice of him to apologize amid all the noise and confusion!

Mary Woolf

Ted Revell, RASC, on the right.

Home Guard Carpenter

In 1939 when I was eleven the war began and my father joined the Home Guard. They met in the Territorial Army Hall. He was put in charge of carpentry although as my mother would say, 'He can only put in a 6-inch nail.'

Mary Ellis

Ten-Ton Roller

The TA building was bombed and me and my mates found some bullets and hand grenades in the wreckage. We sat on the edge of the street and when a big ten-ton roller went past we threw all these explosives under the roller. Well, the roller was undamaged but the bullets rebounded and peppered our legs with bits of metal. We were taken to a local clinic where the bits were plucked out. One of the things I remember clearly was Dad arriving home on a snowy day; with his goggles on he looked like a walking snowman.

Bert Youell

Raids All Round Us

During the Second World War we lived in Glebe Road and as it was near both the Hoffmans and Marconi works, there were raids all round us. In 1943 we were in the Morrison shelter when a blast went through the house, we got our breath back and said, 'Thank God we're alive'. They repaired the houses and we went back later, but some people died in that raid. We all had ration coupons and things were very tight during those years.

Ivy Holden

Commandeered Coaches

My brother who was in the TA was called up early. My father drove for Primrose Coaches and he and his coach were commandeered to drive the Army about. They painted the coach khaki and off he went. As he was not a young man he soon returned home and drove a taxi from then on. On VE Day we ended up in Tindal Square, my mother, my sister and her husband and I. There was music and dancing in the square.

Phyllis Everett

Women's Voluntary Service

My father served some of his Amy time in England before being sent to West Africa and my mother worked at the Model Laundry in Victoria Road. She didn't earn much and often had to take us to a shop the WVS ran in a building near the Ship pub. It was like a swap shop – we handed in clothes that were too small for us and they gave us bigger sizes. I never had any underpants and the coarse grey trousers were very itchy and uncomfortable.

Bert Youell

Barrage Balloon

The old market used to be off the London Road. One day some friends and I were we gathered up all our bits and went into the Morrison shelter in the living room. We used the top as our table. It was like a double bed – you know the old iron ones – and it had bars like a cage round the sides and we all got in until the 'all clear'.

Molly Watson

Admirals Park

We were freezing and my brothers and I used to go out looking for bits of wood to burn on the fire. One day we took Dad's bowsaw. He was very careful with this tool, keeping it wrapped in oily cloths for protection, and he had repeatedly warned us never to touch it. We took our sled and went to Admirals Park to cut down some trees. We had often done the same thing but this time it went wrong. The saw got stuck halfway through a trunk and we were unable to shift it; finally we were forced to give up and go home without the saw, but we knew Dad was going to be mad when he found out. Children whose fathers were in the Armed Services had certain rights. One of these was a Christmas party, which was held in the Victoria Road Hall. It had the normal jelly and blancmange but the thing I remember most was a game of kiss and chase, and the big girl who chased me everywhere!

Bert Youell

Molly's sister Chrissie in the ATS.

amazed to see a barrage balloon right in the middle of the market. We couldn't believe that no one was guarding it and as we were in possession of some safety pins we did our best to pop it. We were most disappointed when nothing happened.

Pat Gillen

Morrison Shelter

During the war when the blackout was in force we bought the black cotton fabric from a shop in Moulsham Street and made our own curtains. I remember the siren going:

Essex Troops Comforts Fund

Mrs Pearce took on voluntary work with the Essex Troops Comfort Fund, with money usually obtained from public collections. She bought wool and distributed it among

ATS girls.

local women so they could knit socks and gloves for the Forces and collecting the items when they were finished. I looked after Valerie while her mother was out and they still had a cleaner to do the housework. Soldiers started to complain that they were getting blisters as the toe of the socks were not properly grafted. I was quite a good knitter and from a book I quickly learnt how to graft. I sat and worked for ages until all the socks were fit to wear.

Ida Cunningham

Corned Beef Pudding

Loftin Way was on the edge of town and after a raid we could look over the town and see where the fires had started. We had an air-raid shelter in the garden, but I remember staying with a friend once and using the shelter under their table. I hated it because I could get no air. In my lunch hour I went round the shops to see what had come in and what they were selling; rationing was on so any little extras you could find you were glad of. Sometimes they would sell a few sweets not on ration – when I got home the family would ask what I had managed to buy. We got an allowance of corned beef each week and I'd make a meat pudding with it. We grew our own vegetables as we had a big garden, we had 2oz butter, 2oz margarine, a little sugar and one egg per person. We could get dried egg that came from America: it was lovely and made great scrambled egg.

Doris Wesley

Recycled Ration Coupons

We all had ration books and food was hard to come by. My two mates, Barry Patience and Mick Riley, and myself worked out that when the shopkeeper took the coupons he must have had to hand them in elsewhere, so we finally traced them to an office in Wells Street. We shinned up the drainpipe, went in through a window and helped ourselves to a load of coupons. We passed these around the neighbourhood and the mothers fixed them in their books and managed to use them again. Children were told to take empty jam jars to school occasionally and the teachers would share out a big sack of chocolate powder; when we were in the office in Wells Street we had seen several of these sacks along one of the walls. Some were full of chocolate powder and the others full of sugar. I think it was when we went back for some more chocolate that we got caught. The policeman marched me down to the police station threatening all sorts of terrible things along the way but when we reached the station he just slapped my head and sent me on my way.

Bert Youell

Library List

The bomb at Hoffmans was bad. We went to the Civic Centre which was then the library to look at the lists to see who was alive or dead.

Mary Woolf

An Employment Registration card.

Doodlebugs

When the war was on each day was an adventure. Clothes were on coupons and I would save up and go to the market. We had a Morrison shelter in the front room. A bomb hit the gas pipe nearby and flames were everywhere outside. A doodlebug hit Park Avenue and a whole shower of incendiaries came down Swiss Avenue. On VE Day there was a party in Dixon Avenue and we saw everyone having fun.

Mary Ellis

Gas Mask Fitting

Before war was declared I remember going to be fitted for a gas mask. When I went to a Girl Guide camp in 1939 we had to take our masks with us. They were taken from us and packed in a wooden box to be kept safe and then returned to us so we could take them home.

We had blackout curtains. My brother-in-law was an ARP warden; his post was under the library (this is now the Civic Centre). When a raid was reported he would patrol out of doors on the alert for fire bombs. Some fell on the path at the bottom of our garden.

Phyllis Everett

Coded Streamers

As an Army messenger my father sometimes came close to Chelmsford and he took every opportunity to come home and see us. He was home one night when a barrage balloon came down over Railway Street. It was moving fast and causing damage, and when some chap tried to slow it down by grabbing the cable, it didn't slow it at all and he lost all the skin of his hand. The wire cables were very strong and very thick. There was a lot of aerial activity that night – several decoy balloons as well as enemy planes. We saw the American bombers coming back; they had coded colours and flew streamers so their ground crew could be prepared if they had a problem, like a damaged plane or an injured man – I didn't know what colours meant what.

Bert Youell

5th Essex Regiment

I had joined the TA so had to report in 1939. Only two others in my department at Hoffmans were called up at the same time. During the war I was in the 2nd Battalion 5th Essex Regiment and after Dunkirk I was transferred to the training centre at Great Barr, Birmingham, so in 1940 after all the losses I had to train new recruits. I then volunteered for the Royal Artillery Maritime Regiment; they were used on both merchant and troop ships for anti-aircraft defence. I was there until the end of the war.

Dennis Smith

Signals Operator

In early 1940 when I was eighteen and a half I joined the RAF. Initially I went to West Drayton and then to radio school at Cranwell. I trained as a signals operator before being sent to 3 Group Bomber Command at Newmarket and then to Y Service at Chicksands Priory in Bedfordshire, where we worked in connection with Bletchley Park. I later moved to 1 Group Bomber Command in

Dennis and Mollie Smith, 1943.

interested in the cord. It was thick woven silk and came in different colours, much sought after on the swapping rounds. The perspex was often made into rings and jewellery but we made it into catapult handles. At school the teachers gave us three different coloured tickets. They marched us to a large shed-like building that used to stand in Victoria Road, where the WVS ran a sort of canteen for poorer children. It was one ticket each for dinner, pudding and a drink. They served a lot of macaroni cheese – I didn't like it then and I don't like it now.

Bert Youell

Hoffman's Ball Bearings

There was no air-raid shelters in our school and when the sirens went off over Chelmsford we had to sit in the main corridor until the 'all clear'. The nuns made sure we took our work with us and didn't waste our time while we were sitting in the corridor. I remember seeing the shocked faces of people at the time the workers at Hoffmans Ball Bearings were attacked; they were either strafed by machine guns from a low-flying fighter or they had been bombed, I can't remember which. I think it must have happened as they were leaving work and some people were killed.

Pat Gillen

Yorkshire before returning to 3 Group and then being demobbed. When on leave I came back to my parents home in Chelmer Road; I remember visiting the Corn Exchange for dancing to live bands. I bought clothes at Bond's with coupons.

Barbara Rayment

Catapult Handles

We rushed there on our bikes: a V2 had landed in the fields and hadn't exploded. Everyone was after the parachute and the perspex; the silk from the parachute was good for clothes but as boys we were more

Marconi Huts Explosion

During the war I remember going into an air-raid shelter near the library. We had an

Anderson shelter at home. There were no street lights allowed so it was very dark when I was going home after my work in the florist. Marconi's had some huts at the end of Sunrise Avenue where we lived and one day an explosive was dropped on the huts.

Gladys Hilliard

Unexploded Bomb

In Tenfield Street a German mine took out every house in the whole street and an unlucky customer at the Steamer pub who was enjoying his pint of beer outside was killed by a stray bullet. A girl at school called Daphne Robinson lived in Glebe Road, she told us that she had a space ship in her back garden and if we became friends of hers we could see it. We all wanted to be her friend and after school we went to play with this big silver space ship, it was between six and seven foot long and we climbed all over it sat on top of it and had a load of fun. On our way to school next morning we saw that the whole area around Glebe Road had been evacuated and fenced off – our space ship was a 500lb unexploded bomb.

Bert Youell

Mrs Cullis

Hoffmans had a big canteen; Mrs Cullis was in charge and she did very good meals. She would do fruit tart and rice pudding in big bowls like washing up bowls – they were absolutely delicious. They served no end of lunches and during the war turned the ballroom into a canteen as the old one was too small for all the workers.

Doris Wesley

Beaufort Guns

They tried to teach me how to drive a horse and cart. They loaded the cart with turnips and said, 'You'll have to say "walk on" and he'll go.' Before I could say anything to the horse a Beaufort gun went off. Like a shot he was off with me holding on for dear life, with turnips falling out of the back. People shouted 'Whoa!' but he took no notice and went straight to the farm where he was supposed to go. The Beaufort guns were in a field on the other side of the road from where the college had a farm; they were somewhere near Lawford Lane where Marconi's was. We never knew when they were going to go off so we would say a prayer as we went in the fields to work. We never had any glass shattered but the greenhouses would shake with the noise and you'd think they were going to collapse. We would also watch the dog fights in the sky.

Mary Woolf

Bomb Shelters

When we were in Coval Lane we didn't have a shelter and had to go under the stairs in the kitchen when the air-raid siren went. In Tudor Avenue there was a shelter at the end of the road for residents who wanted to go to it; those in the lower flats had a Morrison shelter – this had a big flat surface like a table with grid walls on all sides, and

Listening to an old-fashioned record player.

the last one you pulled in behind you. We shared with our neighbours: mum, me, my sister, the neighbour and her baby. We perfected the art of getting in: I went in first and was in the corner, then my sister followed by my mother and the neighbour with her baby. Father never went in the Morrison shelter but sometimes he went into the one at the end of the road for a chat. They liked him going there because he cheered everyone up.

Phyllis Everett

Internal Emergency Warning

At Hoffmans when the air raid siren went we had to go to the air-raid shelters down the back of the factory. We played cards and so on in there, so as you can imagine we took our time when the 'all clear' sounded! So then they said we had to get under our desks if the internal emergency warning went – that was activated if the watchers saw enemy aircraft coming round. There were no lights in any of the streets, all were pitch black. We would go to social evenings and cycle home in the dark but we thought nothing of it. To learn anything about the progress of the war you had to listen to the radio or read the newspapers.

Doris Wesley

Air-Raid Shelters

The Civic Centre had a big cellar which was used as a shelter. It held between fifty and sixty people and the concrete garden shelters held up to twelve people, so if your family didn't have one you could join a neighbour in theirs. If a bomb landed near enough to these concrete shelters it could be overturned, risking trapping the people inside. To avoid this a diamond-shaped escape hole was built in, using soft bricks and loose mortar that could easily be pushed out in an emergency. A doodlebug landed on the roof of the Eastern National bus station; it didn't go off and the area was evacuated until it was disposed of in the safest manner. I was still only twelve when the war finished; to me at that age it was like one big adventure.

Bert Youell

Open Party

In Duke Street we could see all that happened on VE Day. The Corn Exchange relayed music and it was one big open party. The Americans came into town; they would pick any girl up and swing her round in the air, everyone was so excited. I loved music, especially Deanna Durbin whose records I played on my gramophone. When we heard the German planes going over I used to get so frightened that I would put on the record of Deanna Durbin singing 'Ave Maria'.

Mary Woolf

HMS Christie

When a big bomb went off it left a large crater perhaps thirty or forty feet deep. One that we played in had filled with water, so we dragged an old water tank there, wrote 'HMS Christie' on the side and climbing in launched ourselves into the flooded crater. The heavy tank turned turtle and we were trapped underneath. I was really scared and I still don't know how we managed to get out.

Bert Youell

CHAPTER 7

Fashion

Douglas Catt with his parents.

A Little Boy in a Satin Suit

I married in 1940 at All Saints' church. I wore a long white dress that had been made for me. I carried variegated carnations and had two bridesmaids who wore blue flowered dresses, a little girl in a long pale blue dress and a little boy in a satin suit. He was only between eighteen months and two years old and as he walked through the church he looked up and this caused him to fall over backwards. We had our reception in the County Hotel and he spent all his time in the ladies' room looking at himself in the mirror. My father wore a bowler hat and his best suit and my mother wore a navy blue suit and a hat. Reverend Hargreaves officiated; he later went to Beverley Minster, near York. As my husband and I both worked at Hoffmans we had two days off for our honeymoon. We went to the cinema in Brentwood and saw Bing Crosby and Bob Hope.

Ivy Holden

A Bootlace Tie

As a teenager I was a Teddy Boy. I wore 3-inch high spongy soled shoes with blackish suede uppers, and drainpipe trousers of a gabardine material. My jacket was three-quarter length, with very wide lapels of a blackish velvet, which I wore over a smart white shirt and a thin bootlace tie. I had the DA hairstyle held rigidly in place by my home-made gel – like other lads I mixed eau de Cologne with liquid paraffin then massaged it into my hair, and it set solid.

Bert Youell

A Personal Axe

The first tunic we had in the early days was made of Melton, a dark navy tunic buttoned to the neck. They had trials later to try to find a better tunic material, but to start with nothing bettered it, the others all fried. Later they came up with a better product, and we wore fire trousers, leggings, fireboots and a helmet. We all had a black leather belt with a personal axe and belt line, all of which had to be polished. The axe was in a buttoned-over pouch.

Doug Pheasant

Camiknickers

We tried to follow the fashion but I never wore a hat although I was envious of those that wore hats with style. Fashion during the war was to wear a georgette or chiffon scarf round the head then tuck the hair in all round. We had the old home perm sets and we wore lisle stockings until nylon came in.

Fine lisle stockings were very strong but there wasn't much choice. I made slips and French knickers; we had parachute silk if you could get it to make them. Also camiknickers, which were slip and knickers all in one.

Doris Wesley

Miss Muppet Cotton Material

I did a lot of needlework. The first sewing machine I had was a toy one, and then I had a machine my mum bought me from a rummage sale. It only did a chain stitch and there was no bobbin so if you let go of the cotton you lost the lot. My husband's mother later gave me a Singer Treadle with a case on the top – it was a wonderful machine, nothing like the modern ones you get today. I would send away for Miss Muppet cotton material for children, it cost $6\frac{1}{2}$ d a yard. I knitted a lot and bought wool in the Scotch Wool shop next to Grippers; from the same shop I would also buy paper patterns that I ironed on to material which I embroidered with Anchor silks. I embroidered cushion covers and all sorts of things including a tapestry seat for a chair, that lasted for many years.

Sally Pattendon

A Halo Hat

The market was outside and most of the stallholders came from London. On a Friday people queued to buy the latest styles – it was so much cheaper than in the shops. Of course we wore hats; you weren't dressed without a hat. There were cloches and very, very fashionable Halos – you pulled them on and

A fashionable hat.

they went up in the front: all the fashionable young girls had a Halo. Gloves were a must and fur collars, and it really was fur in them days. Fox fur was the cat's whiskers and if you couldn't afford a fox you had a beaver one. Astrakhan was fashionable and court shoes, plain black patent.

Molly Watson

Hats and Hair

In the early days I usually did my hair myself but sometimes went to a hairdresser in Victoria Road near where 'The Back Inn Time' is now. I would have my hair cut short but later did a lot of back-combing when bouffants came in. If I ever wore a hat it was a little skull cap or a beret except in the WAAF, of course, when I wore my peaked cap.

Grace Pheasant

Co-op Outfitters

I never had a school uniform; we wore ordinary clothes and most went to school in a jacket. I was too old to be a Teddy Boy by the time that became fashionable. I bought most of my clothes from the Co-op who had a good men's outfitters, on the corner of Baddow Road. Of course there was always Fosters.

David Cook

Green Eye Shadow

In the sixties, capes were very fashionable; I had a camel-coloured one. Also fashionable were stiletto shoes with pointed toes, fishnet stockings and like most other young girls I would back-comb my hair for hours to achieve the highest bouffant style possible. I usually used Boots No. 7 medium range makeup, bright green eye shadow with pencil line inside the rim of my eye and thick mascara. My underwear came from Marks & Spencer's – of course there was no C&A in Chelmsford. I think the nearest store was in Ilford.

Margaret Brannan

The Tallyman

My grandmother lived with us in Chignal. She made a lot of our clothes, all by hand, although

Wedding of Douglas Catt's parents.

her fingers were bent with rheumatism. She would cut down my father's old trousers and remake them for us. My mother bought some clothes from the tallyman who came to the door; his name was Mr Clark and he came from Bishop's Stortford. Mother paid him 2s 6d a week, or whatever she could afford. At the end of the year the tallyman would knock something off the bill – for example if it was £3 he would perhaps knock off £2.

Ted Revell

Black Market

I made all my own clothes and have always had a sewing machine. I inherited one from my mother and my step-mother was an expert dressmaker and helped me; I also went to classes. During the war we tried to get material not on ration through the black market – it was vyella type material, and you could also buy vyella with coupons. I also knitted all our jumpers of course. After the war I would buy my material to make the children's clothes at the market or at Smith's – they sold everything, it was a lovely shop. I would also buy patterns there it was a good old fashioned shop. Bonds was another source but usually I liked going to the market. Crimplene came and was very popular as it is so easy to work with.

Doris Wesley

Grace in her 'Mary Pickford' dress

Pill Box Hat

After the war in 1947 we adopted a little girl. We moved to Writtle Road when she was eighteen months old. I made clothes for my daughter but not for myself; my mother made all my dresses on her Singer sewing machine, a hand-operated one. I remember a little pillbox hat I had, but I only wore hats to weddings and to church.

Ivy Holden

Mary Pickford's Dress

I was a driver in the WAAF based at RAF Valley on the Isle of Anglesey when I first met Doug, my husband-to-be. We got married in 1945 between VE Day and VJ Day at Holy Trinity church in Barkingside, the town I came from. The wedding dress I wore had belonged to the American film star Mary Pickford; she and other film stars donated these dresses to the WAAF. After the wedding it had to be packaged up ready for the next WAAF wedding.

Grace Pheasant

Pipe Cleaners

We all grew our hair and had it in Shirley Temple ringlets or little sausage-like rolls all round the back. We couldn't afford the steel curlers that you could buy at Woolworth's as they were rather expensive – sixpence, which was a lot of money – so we bought pipe cleaners which we bent in half before rolling our hair in them. We tucked the ends under, then slept in them, of course. In the morning we slid out the pipe cleaners, rolled our hair round a finger, and then had lovely big sausage curls all along the back and up the side.

Molly Watson

The Melton Uniform

By the time I got married in 1961 my wage had risen to £4 a week. My wife came from Braintree and we got married but it was a long while before I earned £20 a week. We were allocated two uniforms after completing our training as firemen: one was our fire-fighting gear and the other was called the off-duty set. We reported for parade at the start of our duty in our fire

Swimsuits of yesteryear. Molly Watson is on the right.

Firemen in dress uniform.

The Rusbys' wedding day.

A Burton Suit

In 1935 when I started as a messenger boy at the brigade, I was given a khaki overall to wear but it was heavy like a coat. Chelmsford Council soon sent me to Burton's menswear in the High Street for a special suit, good trousers and a warm button-up coat. I wore this suit until I was sent for training and became a fireman when of course I received my proper uniforms. Most of the men were retained; this meant they did their ordinary jobs and ran for duty to the station when they heard the fire siren.

Harold Wakelin

kit and reported on parade at the end of duty in our off-duty kit. The officer in charge of the station took the parades and allocated each man to their particular engine for that shift. Once you knew your place you put your gear on the engine ready to hand for any emergency. If you were lucky you received a pre-war uniform: they were warm, comfortable and made from Melton. Later the uniforms were made out of a heavy serge with a 1½-inch deep dog collar that had a two-hook fastening. This was very uncomfortable to wear and much too hot. The off-duty uniform was made from a lighter weight material and easier to wear.

Dave Wright

CHAPTER 8

Transport

Red Watch with Lynne Harding.

Bradwood Body

I had to pass the brigade driving test before I could drive the fire engines. I was able to do this fairly soon after my training course. I drove the engines for thirty years and only had one minor scrape in that time. When I started the station had one pre-war machine called a 'Bradwood Body' and one ex-Army engine. The Bradwood Body was the type where the firemen sat along the sides. As soon

as the bell went we jumped on the side, making sure we held on to the bar with one hand, our elbow dug as deep as possible behind the bar, while with the other hand we dressed in our fire-fighting kit as the engine sped through the streets towards the emergency. Later on we were upgraded and got some Dennis machines. These had Rolls Royce engines and were very fast, great engines, but finally they had to be replaced and in the late '50s or early '60s the service

Fire engine, between 1915 and 1920.

was offered several Dodge engines at a reduced price. They were alright but not as good as the Rolls Royce engines.

Dave Wright

Little Green MG

When I was a teenager not many girls drove cars, though I suppose they were just starting to then. One of my boyfriends had a little green MG. It looked good but was really ropy. He paid about £70 for it and with a lot of tinkering about managed to use it for quite some time. If he was unable to start it by cranking it up with the starting handle, we would have to push it; we would try to go fast enough to get into a run and when the engine turned over we had to jump in quickly and then we were off. Another friend had a BSM motorcycle which cost well over £100 and was in very good condition. I often rode on the pillion. In those days it was not necessary to wear helmets or special protective clothing – I think we were unaware of the dangers involved. In the summer we just wore cotton trousers and tops with a pair of sandals; we often rode in groups and I don't remember anyone having helmets or gloves.

Mary Scott

Austin Ruby

When I first met my husband he had an Austin Ruby. We drove down to Devon in that. In 1939 – which was before we were married – we had a black Ford. It cost £100 and we kept it in the garage until we were bombed out; we couldn't use it of course because there was no petrol. Later we had another Ford but I didn't learn to drive until 1955.

Ivy Holden

Ford Consul

My mum bought me my first bike – it cost about £4 and she paid cash for it; she never bought things any other way. The first car I bought was a dark blue Austin Seven. I had saved up for a long while and Mum and Dad helped me pay for it. I drove that Austin for three or four years before trading it in for a Ford Consul.

Harold Wakelin

Hospital Bus

I cycled everywhere up to two years ago. When I was young I always cycled to work although when I went to church I usually managed to get a lift. I did use the bus if the weather was bad – the hospital bus has been running for as long as I can remember.

Gladys Hilliard

Sit Up and Beg Bike

When I started work I had to get from Kelvedon to Chelmsford. This meant being in Witham by 6.40 in the morning to catch the bus that ran from there to Hoffmans. I had never ridden a bike so I bought a sit up and beg cycle on the never-never and taught myself to ride. It was the only way I had of getting to Witham at that time in the morning. It was the same in the evening when I left work – I caught the 5.15 p.m. Eastern National outside the works into Witham then cycled to Kelvedon, arriving home after 6 p.m. In the summer I sometimes cycled all the way to Chelmsford and parked my cycle in Newcomes Garage.

Prior to the war at twelve mid-day and in the evening you could see up to three hundred cyclists in New Street, through the town and up the High Street, then along Rectory Road as they cycled home.

Dennis Smith

Rover 80

My main mode of transport in the early years was my bicycle. As a child I cycled to school and later to work and when I joined the RAF the first thing I got was a bicycle and the last thing you handed in when you left was your bike. Later I had an Austin 55 and then a super old car, a Rover 80, which I had for over six years. It had a bench seat and our dog would lie along it with his head on my thigh.

Doug Pheasant

Moores School Bus

We went to school by bus; there were about six of us from Witham. We went on a Moores bus – sometimes they sent a single-decker and sometimes a double-decker bus. The drivers were very good, kind and considerate, and I remember Miss Bishop who taught music or French at the Priory came on the bus and kept an eye on everyone. She was very nice and did her job well. At the weekends if the right guard was working we used to get a free ride from Witham to Chelmsford on the footplate of the steam trains; we then waited at Chelmsford station, which of course was much quieter than it is now, until we found a guard willing to give us a free ride back. It

Fred Underwood in his Wolseley.

was a wonderful feeling riding on those footplates.

Pat Gillen

Frederick Underwood

My mother's father Frederick Underwood built a house next to the County Hotel, called Elm Trees. This house is now part of the County Hotel itself. Grandfather Underwood was one of the first people in Chelmsford to own a motor car – it was a Wolseley, I think. My father bought a motorbike and later a motor car; it was a 1913 Standard with a dickey seat, and on early closing day Wednesday we would drive to Heybridge Basin, Braintree or Southend. Around ten miles was as far as we would drive.

Douglas Catt

Ford Prefect

I learnt to drive a car before I went in the Army. I was taught to drive by a chap who owned the Oxney Green garage, I passed the test in Chelmsford then later passed another one in the Army for heavy goods vehicles. I bought my first car in 1959 or 1960. It was a Ford Prefect and cost £50 from Burns in Broomfield Road. I sold it for £50 and bought a Morris 1000 Traveller for £145 which I sold a year later for £150 before buying an Austin A40 from Broomfield Road Garage.

Ted Revell

1933 Morris 12

When I was a teenager I had different types of motorized cycles, the sort where the motor was fitted to either the front or the

114

back wheels. I had a French one called an Autovac and another called a Mini Motor. I also had a new Hudson moped which cost me £30. It wasn't necessary to pass a driving test for small motors and they didn't use much petrol. My first car was sold to me by the bank manager when he was getting a new one – it was a 1933 Morris 12 and cost me £10 10s. I drove that for about four years before replacing it with a Hillman Minx.

Bert Youell

Bus, Ferry and Train

As a child I was taken to Kent for holidays. We would go to Tilbury by bus and then cross by ferry to Gravesend and either take the train to Deal or the bus to Strood.

Ivy Holden

A Bike for under £5

Not many people had cars. I had my first bike aged thirteen years and it cost under £5. There was a regular bus service to Writtle through Beehive Lane. I had my first bus ride in 1928 when I was five; strangely enough they were small buses like they put on now, with no conductors. It was Eastern National as it is now and also Pattern's Coaches.

David Cook

Princes Road

When younger I relied on public transport, sometimes travelling to London on the train. Moulsham Street and London Road were the main routes for buses and coaches. Princes Road was built in 1932. Although I

Learning to drive in the 1960s.

Cycle and car in the 1960s

taken from their stables behind The Bell Hotel in Tindal Street to the nearby station, they were backed into the shaft at the front of the engine, then off they trotted to the fire. That engine was still outside the back of the station many years after it was no longer in use.

Harold Wakelin

Austin 10

I passed my driving test when I was twenty-one and bought an Austin 10, a black one – they were all black then – and it cost me £70 second-hand. I had that car for six months before it was stolen; it turned up in Broomfield sand pits.

George Christodoulou

Chelmsford Borough Council

As a mechanic with Chelmsford Borough Council I had a variety of jobs. I worked on the traffic lights, at sewage stations as well as repairing dustcarts and other council vehicles. I lived at 35 Lady Lane a in a council worker's house. It backed on to the council yard and I only had to step through a hole in the fence and I was home. In the '50s I was paid £4 10s for a 48-hour week, which was quite good money then.

Bert Youell

The £300 Austin

We cycled most places; my daughter would be on the back of my bike and my husband

walked to work I did have a bicycle and sometimes cycled with friends. The future King George VI came to open Princes Road in 1932. all the school children were taken; my brother went but I was ill. Later the Queen came to Chelmsford and I was ill then too. I never saw rRoyalty as I was indisposed!

Phyllis Everett

Steam Fire Engine

In 1935 the fire engines still had solid rubber tyres and it was a really bouncy ride. A few years later I drove a Metz, which was a German appliance with a turntable and extending ladder. There used to be an old steam fire engine. I remember my father responding to the siren: the two horses were would have my son on the crossbar. When I was young during the war in the summer we used to go down to Mill Beach on Sundays (as other coastal areas were restricted). Eight or so Hoffmans apprentices and their girlfriends would cycle down there. It cost nothing as we would take our food and stop for a drink on the way back. I relied on my bike for travel but used public transport for longer journeys. In about 1965 we bought an Austin for about £300 and we went all over England in it.

Doris Wesley

A Car for £20

I had my first car in 1965. It was an Austin 10 and I paid £20 for it. I did over 10,000 miles and it never let me down. It had lovely leather seats, as I recall. Before that I cycled everywhere; when my wife was ill in Black Notley I cycled the twelve miles there and twelve miles back. We could only visit Wednesday and Sunday so if I was on duty I could not go.

Pete Huckle

Austin 7

I travelled mostly by cycle but my father had an Austin 7 in which he would travel backwards and forwards from the nurseries in Writtle to his shop in Duke Street. He used it to carry seeds, plants, vegetables, made-up floral displays and other produce that he sold.

Mary Woolf

A pre-war garage forecourt.

Charabanc

We liked to cycle and would ride all round the countryside. I went swimming a lot in the outdoor pool in Chelmsford and taught my children to swim there too. I remember as a child catching a charabanc outside the Barn pub to go and visit relatives in Haverhill. I was a bad traveller so had to sit on a pile of newspapers and covered myself in scent and my father took along a bucket of sand.

Mary Ellis

The Ammunition Dump

During the war I would catch a train to Liverpool Street station. They were steam trains then and as safe as houses. When I was stationed in Shropshire I worked on the biggest ammunition dump in this country. It supplied all our invasion forces with ammunition – nitroglycerine was the highest explosive before the atom bomb. We loaded it on to trains to be delivered to all the different ports and those steam trains never had one accident.

Ted Revell

Brass Lamp

I saw my first car when I used to walk to Springfield School. It belonged to a man called Mr Pledger who lived near New Hall and he passed us on his way home. It was an open car with brass lamps at the front and it went so slowly we used to walk along beside him. Springfield was a village then – just the church and some big houses.

Ivy Holden

250 BSA Motorcycle

When I started work in Chelmsford I caught the bus; it cost 2s 6d for a day return and took about thirty minutes from Dunmow. I think it was cheaper to buy a weekly but I never did. The buses ran more frequently than they do now and were a lot more reliable. I then bought a 250 BSA motorcycle; it had a pillion and cost me about £80 second-hand. I had to apply for petrol coupons so that I could go backwards and forwards to work on it. Before the war the cheapest pedal cycle you could buy cost £3 19s 6d.

Dave Wright

CHAPTER 9
A Medley

Dot at her retirement.

Father Christmas

Being married to a fireman was sometimes difficult when the children were young. I would be on my own and when things went wrong I would have to deal with them. When my husband was off duty we would take the children fishing. My husband's job always had a children's party; Harold Wakelin used to dress up as Santa Claus and I remember his small son at one party saying, 'Father Christmas, you've got legs just like my dad.'

Thelma Huckle

Teddy Boy

When I was a teenager I became a Teddy Boy. There were many rival gangs and other gangs would come to Chelmsford looking for a fight. The Teddy Boys usually carried razors, bike chains, even knuckle dusters. I never used any weapons and was fortunate enough not to be wounded, though many people were, especially with razor cuts. The gang from the Elephant and Castle in London came to Chelmsford; they travelled either by motorbike or on the train and they grouped up outside the Regent Cinema which was the usual place for a punch up.

Bert Youell

Seconded to Cyprus

In 1958 the brigade asked for volunteers who would be prepared to serve in Cyprus for six months. That was at a time of civil unrest over there and as the Cyprus Fire Service was made up of both Greeks and Turks it was decided to have British officers in charge until the emergency was over. We took our own uniforms with us. I was there between September and April and even at that time of year the temperature was in the 70s. Some people from Chelmsford stayed for twelve months but my mum was unwell and I decided to come back at the end of the six months.

Dave Wright

'Giddy Potter'

I remember taking the children in the pushchair to the top of Admirals Park and looking across at the floods – all you could see was the top of the swings. There was a cottage in the field where the Potter family lived. They had a son we called 'Giddy Potter'; when the floods came all the Potters had to be rescued.

Mary Ellis

First Visit to Chelmsford

After our marriage Doug and I lived in married quarters in Cambridgeshire. In 1952, when he came out of the RAF, we moved to Chelmsford. But my first visit to the town had been when I met his mother for the first time several years before. She lived in Wallace Crescent and I went to lunch; the chap next door grew horseradish and on my first visit I took a large helping of this with my meal. It was so strong I was speechless, red in the face and my eyes streaming.

Grace Pheasant

'Dot' The Cook

Dot lived with her son Rex in Forest Drive, Chelmsford. She was quite a character; no-one upsets the cook in a fire station. Assistant Divisional Officer Whybrow presented her with her retirement gift in the late '60s, and several people attended including Pete Huckle, Harry Brender, Mick Hill, George Saunders, Fred Thompson, Jim Sherwin, Percy Prentice, Dave Johnson, Marjory Moss, Wally Broomfield, Lynne Harding, John Smith, Doris Burgess, John Blewett, Roger Hill and Don Hedgecock.

Lynne Harding

The Fumigated Mattress

I had to go into the isolation hospital when I was about twelve as I had scarlet fever. When you had it your mattress had to be taken away and fumigated and then you were taken to the hospital in Baddow Road. I was there for twelve weeks, including Christmas when we had a good time, but parents had to talk to us through windows. I later had my tonsils out in the London Road hospital and was only in for twenty-four hours.

Doris Wesley

Getting a Fair Deal

In 1965 each fire station had their own branch of the Firefighters and Control Staff union. It was by attending these meetings that I got interested in political affairs. I wasn't interested so much in the political parties but for the first time I could see that equality and fairness were aims worth working towards. The fire service had one of the smallest unions and in the '60s I remember we were trying to negotiate better hours and a better shoe and stocking allowance. The crew were very supportive of the control staff once they were persuaded that the argument was just. The older members may have been interested in politics but most of the young ones like me were only interested in getting a square deal.

Lynne Harding

Political Pressure

My friend Helen worked for Chapman Jewellers. She and her husband liked to go to political meetings and one night they went to a Labour party meeting. The next day a man came to see Mr Raven, her boss, and said, 'You want to sack her – she went to a Labour meeting. You don't want people like that working for you.'

Mary Ellis

Threadneedle Street

All the houses down Threadneedle Street were fire houses. Eleven properties were fire station accommodation; the big house near the fire station itself was for the Chief. One of the biggest peacetime fires in Chelmsford was when Ridley's Mill was burnt down. It was full of plastic toys and the fire was huge and could be seen for miles around.

Pete Huckle

Isolation Ambulance

When I was a child I got measles and chicken pox one summer. This was before the National Health service and my parents were presented with a bill which read, 'For professional services and medicine, 12s 6d.' My brother got scarlet fever and went to the Fever Hospital up Baddow Road; they came and fetched him in a special ambulance. The Fever Hospital ambulance was distinctive polished wood. The Fever Hospital building is still there.

Phyllis Everett

Wine Circles

Doug and I had season tickets to watch the wrestling at the Corn Exchange.

Occasionally we missed out if he was on night shift. The last bout finished at 10.30, just in time to have a couple of pints at the nearest pub. We also belonged to the Three Rivers wine circle and met in the basement of the old library. There were lots of wine circles about then and we would visit each other, taking our home-made wines. We entered local and national competitions. I excelled at dry red wine and won many prizes. I made elderberry, damson and sloe, and our white wines weren't bad either. One night we had a Tramps Evening at our circle and invited another club. We all dressed as tramps with our teeth blacked but had forgotten to tell the other club and they turned up in dinner jackets – we had great times there. We made beer at home as well, and one Christmas we removed the cork and it shot out like a steam whistle. The recipe said treat with respect!

Grace Pheasant

Royalty Passing Through

In the 1950s I remember taking the children to the corner of Rectory Lane to see the Queen and Prince Philip going to visit Hoffmans. Earlier when I was a child I saw Queen Mary going through Chelmsford. We stood outside Christy's in Broomfield Road and we had to shout 'hooray' and wave our hands.

Mary Ellis

'The Colonel'

My nickname in the fire service was 'The Colonel'. There was a lot of joking and skylarking amongst us all the time. Meal times were often interrupted and we would have our first course and four hours later eat the dessert. Those not on call would write the names down on paper and put them on the plates so we could eat it later.

Doug Pheasant

Bolingbroke & Wenley's

In the late 1940s the Wenley's building was burnt to the ground. They built the Bolingbroke & Wenley's buildings to replace it and they are now pulling that down and going to replace it with several shop units.

Pat Gillen

Plum Coloured Suit

My mother would make all our clothes; she was a clever seamstress. I remember she made my brother Ron a suit out of her old overcoat; it was plum coloured, and he was showing off to all his friends. This was fine until they went to the toilets; the other lads had fly buttons and poor old Ron just had a willy hole!

Ida Cunningham

Major Incidents

I remember being sent to a major incident in Witham at a seed merchant's. There were umpteen appliances there. The tarmac on the road and a telegraph pole

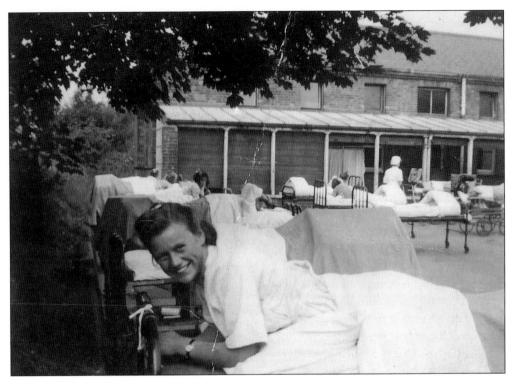

Hospital beds outside in summer.

were burning, it was so fierce. There was a flash over and the roof went. I was still a recruit then and was sent to the river to put pumps in to get water. I was there four hours so saw no more of the fire itself. We attended many road accidents, for which our only equipment was hacksaws and crowbars – none of the sophisticated equipment of today.

Doug Pheasant

The Big Drum

My father always took us out on Sunday morning when my mother was at chapel. We often ended up in the TA Hall in Margaret Road. He played the big drum in

the Essex Regiment and he would go to listen to the band practice.

Mary Ellis

Isolation Hospital

When I was six or seven I was very ill with bronchitis and pneumonia. Dr Whitley of the London Road surgery cycled three and a half miles to our house at ten in the evening; he saved my life. I was sent to Baddow Road Isolation Hospital because they thought I had diphtheria. I hadn't and Dr Whitley apologized to my parents, but I stayed there in an empty ward on my own, except for a nurse who slept with me to keep me company. The wards opposite were the isolation part for diphtheria and scarlet fever. I stayed there for eight weeks. In summer a bed was put outside for me while the nurses played tennis. My older brother visited me; he was handsome and all the nurses wanted to see him. I remember in the ambulance I sat on a nurse's lap and could see the lights of Chelmsford Carnival go by.

Ted Revell

Bob Driver's Scrapyard

When I was in Embankment Terrace the floods came down Victoria Road. To get out of the houses we had to go over the fence and across Bob Driver's scrapyard.

Doris Wesley

Confirmation

I was confirmed in the late '60s at the Cathedral; the Bishop came down to take the classes. My friend Mary Clark who was a Roman Catholic had to get permission to accompany me. I continued going to the Cathedral for a while afterwards and sometimes went to St John's church.

Grace Pheasant

Royal Humane Certificate

When I was in the Dragoons I was on leave and walking hand in hand with my lady friend (later to become my wife), near the river Wid, by the A12 and near the White Horse. In those days it was a wide river. We heard youngsters shouting for help and I saw a young lad in trouble in the water and other boys trying to help him. I dived in and rescued him, a boy of about twelve. An RAC fellow stopped and between us we laid the lad on the RAC box. I jumped on the back and held him on while we all went to the London Road hospital. The RAC driver took me home then kindly took my wet uniform to be cleaned – it was of course that thick old khaki.

Sometime later I was asked specifically to go on church parade the following Sunday. I had no inkling of what was to happen when my CO called me out and to my great surprise I received a certificate from the Royal Humane Society.

Bill Woolley

Cross Keys Huts

My dad was working for Mr Green and we lived in a tied cottage until I was about seven; at that time I went to school in Writtle. We then moved to Roxwell and lived at No. 2 Cross Keys Huts. This was an ex-military camp of some sort that Chelmsford Council used as temporary accommodation. There were lots of families there and I remember some of them as being very large. The children waited outside the Cross Keys pub on the A414 in the mornings and a bus picked us up and took us to school in Roxwell. I loved it there – Dr Coe was the head teacher, a very forward looking man, and they also had a good cook who served up smashing dinners in a sort of canteen.

Lynne Harding

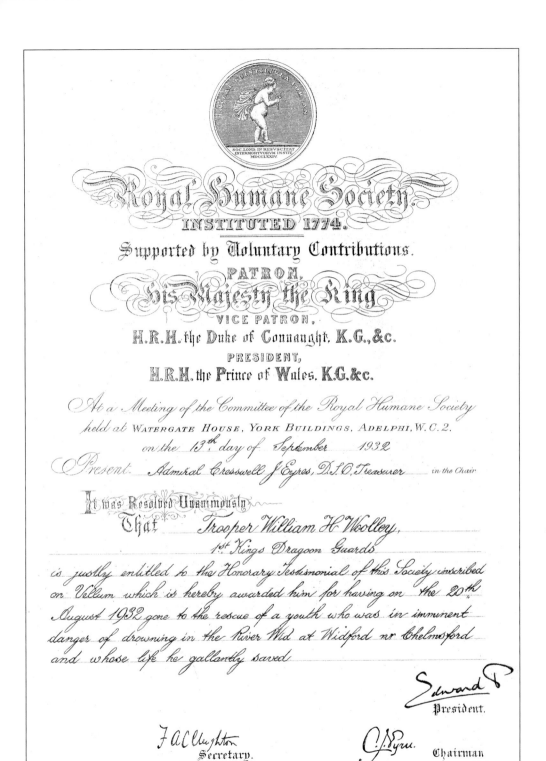

Royal Humane Society.

INSTITUTED 1774.

Supported by Voluntary Contributions.

PATRON,

His Majesty the King

VICE PATRON,

H.R.H. the Duke of Connaught. K.G.,&c.

PRESIDENT,

H.R.H. the Prince of Wales. K.G.&c.

At a Meeting of the Committee of the Royal Humane Society held at WATERGATE HOUSE, YORK BUILDINGS, ADELPHI, W.C.2.

on the 13th day of September 1932

Present. Admiral Cresswell J Eyres, D.S.O. Treasurer   in the Chair

It was Resolved Unanimously

That   Trooper William H Wolley,

1st Kings Dragoon Guards

is justly entitled to the Honorary Testimonial of this Society inscribed on Vellum which is hereby awarded him for having on the 20th August 1932 gone to the rescue of a youth who was in imminent danger of drowning in the River Wid at Widford nr Chelmsford and whose life he gallantly saved

Edward P
President.

J AC Ueughton
Secretary.

C J Pyne
Chairman

51392

Royal Humane Society Certificate.

125

Bert Youell today.

National Service

I was called up for the National Service in 1950. I didn't want to go – I had never been away from my mum and dad before. I caught the train with a few other lads at Chelmsford and as we got nearer to the camp more and more boys got on the train and none of them wanted to go. There were all sorts of escape plots hatched but of course we didn't act on them; we just reported to the camp. I had been employed by Chelmsford Borough Council as a mechanic and an official wrote to the Army requesting that I should be allocated to the maintenance division. I earned about 30s a week but a married man earned £2 10s.

Bert Youell

Mr Harris the Consultant

My brother was quite poorly when he was seven years old and had developed osteomyelitis in a bone of his leg. He went into the children's ward and parents were not allowed in so my father would buy a comic and go to the veranda outside the ward, he would shout out and wave the comic so John would know someone was there. It was nine months before they could see him. There was no penicillin in those days; they opened him up and just put swabs in the wound and the stench was awful. He was in there a long time off and on, and when he came out he had to have a pushchair. Mr Harris, his consultant, lived up the top of London Road. My mother was scared of him. Towards the end of John's treatment, when he was eight, Mr Harris – a very abrupt man – told him to walk across the room. He managed to do that and also to bend his ankle. Mr Harris was surprised and said he hadn't expected him to be able to do all of that. My mother, afraid she might have done something wrong, explained that John had been using my bike. As a consequence Mr Harris used his basement to set up cycle frames so patients could pedal and strengthen their muscles.

Mary Ellis

Found in Chelmsford

During the First World War my sisters and I were separated. I went to an orphanage in Leicester. In 1926 when I was old enough I started looking for them, I heard that they had been sent to Dr Barnardo's in Barkingside. I walked from Leicester to find them, sleeping in barns, working on farms and stealing what food I could. It took me about five days. I finally found them in Chelmsford: all three had been in service and two were now married.

Bill Woolley

Bread Day

Two special days I remember as a child: one was the yearly Co-op children's party, held I believe in a field at the end of Coval Lane. I remember games, buns and a bottle of orange and a lovely sunny day. Another special day was 'Bread Day', when the poorer families once a year went to the Parish Hall and collected bread according to how many were in the family. The bread was lovely and fresh and was handed out by the women of the village.

Ida Cunningham

Widest Spreading Oak in the UK

When I was nine my father was working as a steel erector on Sandon Secondary School when he decided to buy a house and smallholding in that area. The house was on the road to Chelmsford. Sandon was a busy village and famous for having the widest spreading oak tree in the United Kingdom.

Lynne Harding

'Which Way to London'?

Where Rainsford School is now there were fields where we played. My dad had an allotment on the corner of Fox Crescent.

One day a plane landed on the fields and as we ran across a chap in a leather helmet came out and said, 'Which way to London?'

Mary Ellis

Fires and the Cause

In the early days a lot of fires occurred alongside the railway track. They were steam engines then and perhaps some sparks flew out or more often I think the train stokers shovelled out hot embers as the train passed. Grass and moorland often caught fire during the hot weather if people left broken glass or bottles lying around and chimney fires were a big hazard though there were less of these when smokeless fuel became compulsory. It is amazing, but carelessness accounts for about 90 per cent of fires: some people placed electric fires close to their beds, some used blow-lamps to thaw out frozen pipes and managed instead to set the attic alight. There was the odd television set that burst into flames when the sets were full of valves or tubes.

Dave Wright

The Green Shift

At one stage the authorities requested that the firefighters' situation should be looked at. After this, two reports were issued, the Cunningham and the Halroyd. One of these recommended that we should join one of the larger unions, either NALGO or Unison, but we rejected this completely. Chelmsford branch was quite active and once organized a march to County Hall. We also ran a 'work to rule' policy: all

The fire brigade before the First World War.

emergency calls were dealt with promptly but administrative operations were held up. The pay and hours situation never really got resolved until the national strike in the '70s. After this we were allowed to operate a fourth shift; this was called the green and joined white, blue and red the other three shifts.

Lynne Harding

St John's Hospital

I had to go into St Johns Hospital at one time. Mr Pearson was a gynaecologist and his houseman was Dr Banks. At night Dr Banks would play his accordion for us. The ward was heated by three coke-burning stoves. One nurse was a dancer and would entertain us by dancing on the table. Dr Banks later went as a missionary doctor. Canon Wilson of London Road church would visit us in the ward as well as seeing his own parishioners. Sister Bundock was in charge, she was lovely. I had never been in hospital before but I quite enjoyed my time there.

Grace Pheasant